D0119224

Craft Traditions
Classic Techniques
New Projects

CREATIVE
HOME
ARTS
CLUB

Minnetonka, Minnesota

Craft Traditions
Classic Techniques
New Projects

CREATIVE
HOME
ARTS
—CLUB—

Minnetonka, Minnesota

Craft Traditions
Classic Techniques, New Projects

Printed in 2006.

All rights reserved. No part of this publication may be reproduced, stored in an electronic retrieval system or transmitted in any form or by any means (electronic, mechanical, photocopying, recording or otherwise) without the prior written permission of the copyright owner.

Tom Carpenter
Creative Director

Heather Koshiol
Managing Editor

Jennifer Weaverling
Senior Book Development Coordinator

Jenya Prosmitsky
Senior Graphic Designer

Phil Aarrestad
Principal Photographer

Teresa Marrone
Book Production

Bob Green
Assistant Photographer

Maggie Stopera
Stylist

Susan Telleen
Stylist

Contributing writers:
Sue Banker
Marie Browning
Nazanin S. Fard
Jana Freiband
Zoe Graul
Teresa Henn
Nancy Hoerner
Cheryl Natt
Cheryl Nelson
Margaret Hanson-Maddox
Lorine Mason
Nancy Maurer
Monica Tikkanen
Linda Wyszynski

Special thanks to:
Connie Bastyr
Terry Casey
Janice Cauley
Sam Lehman
Happi Olson

3 4 5 6 7 8 9 10 / 10 09 08 07 06
© 2006 Creative Home Arts Club
ISBN 1-58159-243-4

Creative Home Arts Club
12301 Whitewater Drive
Minnetonka, MN 55343
www.creativehomeartsclub.com

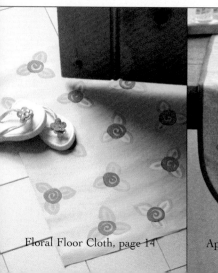

Floral Floor Cloth, page 14

Appliqué Table Runner, page 40

Handmade Greeting Card, page 64

Unique Gift Cards, page 80

Contents

Wire and Bead Earrings, page 98

Dried Floral Wreath, page 108

Bicolor Throw Pillow, page 136

Soap Petals, page 144

Introduction

We've filled our world with high technology, modern conveniences … and unbelievably busy schedules. That means it's more important than ever to slow down and reflect on the simplicity of times gone by. As someone who loves to create beautiful things with their hands, you know the value of stepping back, taking stock, and honoring the traditions of the crafters who came before us.

That's what *Craft Traditions* is all about. These brilliantly colorful pages will bring you back to the "real world" of crafting with *Classic Techniques* you can use on great *New Projects*. Here's everything you need to create some of your most beautiful craft items and decorating accents ever.

Start with essential background on the tools, materials and techniques you'll need to master eight traditional and fun crafting disciplines, including decorative painting, sewing for décor and crafts, needle arts, paper crafts and scrapbooking, jewelry and beading, floral arranging, knitting, and candle and soap making.

Across these eight exciting chapters, you'll find 55 projects that will help you put your new-found skills to work right now on these old-time crafts! Full-color photos guide you every step of the way, so success is assured. You'll even see how much each project might cost you, with the $ (under $10), $$ ($10 to $19) and $$$ ($20 and up) flag that is included with every idea.

It's time to start some new *Craft Traditions* around your home and at your work-table. Let's get crafting … and back to the beautiful basics!

CREATIVE
HOME
ARTS
—CLUB—

Decorative Painting

Decorative painting includes painting for the home, painting crafts and decorative arts or folk art.

Painting for the home and painting crafts share many techniques and products, while folk art reflects historic, regional painting traditions from many diverse cultures, each involving specific techniques and distinctive designs. Many of these designs include flowers, leaves, fruit, bows and sometimes animals. Many folk art styles have remained fairly true to form, even with advanced brushes and updated designs. Popular one-stroke painting methods make it easier than ever to paint traditional designs. Whether you're interested in rosemaling (traditionally painted with oil on wood) or tole (painted using artist's acrylic or oil paints), you may benefit from taking a class or watching a video to help you learn folk art methods.

Paint

Spray paints—as well as spray lacquers and aerosol sealants often used for crafts—are typically available in matte, semigloss and glossy finishes. Latex paints for interior walls, trim, ceilings and floors are also available in a variety of finishes. For high traffic areas and decorative floor cloths, use floor paint sealed with a durable latex urethane finish. Although oil-based paint is available for interior use, it's rarely used due to environmental concerns, a much longer drying time and messier cleanup than latex. Do not layer oil paint over latex paint or vice versa; doing so can cause paint layers to separate and peel.

For craft projects, you will find acrylic paints available in small volumes and with broad color selections.

You will find all your craft and specialty paints at craft stores.

Ceramic paints and ceramic paint pens can be heat-hardened in a low-temperature oven for water resistance, adhesion and durability. For using on glass, try faux stained glass paints or etching mediums for painting on glass. Other specialty paints available at craft stores include fabric paints, 3-D acrylic paints, glitter paints and paint pens.

Manufacturers offer a wide variety of paint, spray paint and additive products for decorative painting. You

Texturizing products add creativity and fun to your craft.

plywood with water-soluble dyes. Aerosol craft primers will seal glass, plastic, ceramic and almost any surface; they will also ensure that paint will adhere to the object.

Before you start any painting project, make sure the surface you intend to paint is clean and smooth. Preparation methods vary depending on the surface material. Clean most surfaces to remove any grease or dirt. Remove old paint or stain with products available to do so. For wood, sand rough spots and remove sanding dust with a clean, damp cloth or a tack cloth. Dust wallboard and

unglazed pottery with a small broom or a vacuum with a soft brush attachment. Clean metal surfaces with lacquer thinner or vinegar, then use sandpaper or a wire brush to remove gloss and rust, and finish preparation by wiping with a clean damp cloth. Before painting on fabric, prewash the fabric if it is washable.

Tools and Techniques

The technique you choose—as well as the type of paint itself—will determine the tools you need for your decorative painting project. General supplies may include tape for masking off areas,

can easily add texture with products like spray pebble or stone, suede or terra-cotta, patina or antiquing kits, sand additives, blending or glazing mediums, colored glazes and textile mediums. For a unique touch, try chalkboard paint, fluorescent paint or glow-in-the-dark paint, all available in liquid or spray form. Check your home improvement or specialty paint stores for information about decorative painting plus paint chips showing color combinations and techniques. Don't forget to inquire about specific tools needed for specialty paint application.

Surface Preparation

When you paint any surface, your preparation impacts your outcome. Always use a primer on new surfaces, porous surfaces or surfaces that will prevent paint from adhering to them (metal, glass or plastic, for example). Use a latex primer for wood or unfinished wallboard, or if you plan to use a paint color that is drastically different from what's already on the surface. A rust inhibiting primer can prevent rust and help paint adhere better to metals. Used to prevent stains from bleeding through new paint, stain-killing primer also works well for knotholes, cedar or

Specific surface designs call for specific tools.

rollers (available in many sizes and textures) and various forms of brushes or applicators. For latex and acrylic paints, use synthetic bristle brushes. If you plan to stencil, you'll find stencil brushes in many sizes made with natural or synthetic bristles. You can create specific design effects with specialty artist's brushes (fan, liner and flat brushes, for example). Foam or sponge applicators—popular, inexpensive and disposable—allow you to avoid visible brush strokes. At paint stores and home centers, you will also find a broad array of special tools including textured, stipple and rag rollers as well as natural sponges, combs and various brushes for texturizing.

To create even more decorative looks, combine the standard decorative painting techniques outlined below. Use these techniques for walls, floors, trim, furniture, accessories and craft items.

For most techniques, you start with a colored base coat that will show. These examples feature contrasting colors to illustrate effects more clearly, but subtle contrasts work well, too.

Experiment with color and tone combinations. (It's a good idea to practice first!) Adding either clear or colored glaze to paint or directly to the surface helps create more depth. More important, a glaze medium will keep latex paint from drying too fast, giving you more time to manipulate the paint. When working with glaze on walls, it's best to work in areas about 3 by 3 feet, so that the glaze does not dry before completion.

The simple technique of sponging actually offers plenty of variations in itself. You can sponge on, using a sponge to apply paint or colored glaze directly to a surface. Sponge one or a few colors onto a base coat. You can sponge off, rolling a layer of paint or glaze over a base coat and then using a sponge to remove some of the top

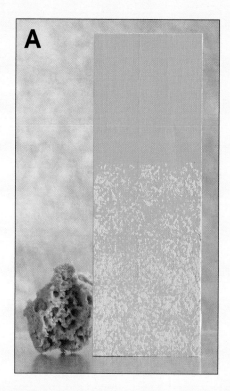

coat. Utilizing a glaze medium will offer more depth. This photo illustrates the effect of sponging on without glaze, using a natural sea sponge (photo A).

Ragging produces an irregular pattern. As with sponging, you can rag on or

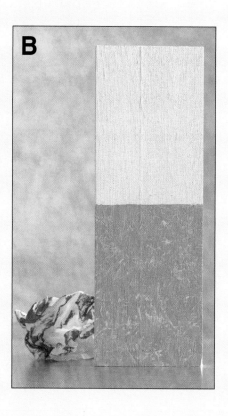

rag off. While a purchased rag roller will result in a more uniform design, using a crumpled soft paper towel, a cotton rag or plastic wrap will yield similar effects (photo B).

Colorwashing—a fairly fast technique—makes a good choice for larger areas. Effects can range from subtle to dramatic. One method of colorwashing involves painting a layer with glaze,

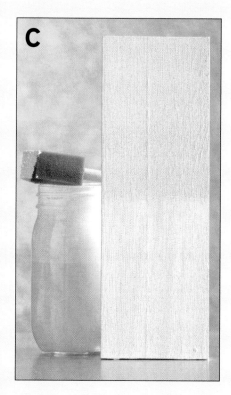

allowing the surface to dry and using a soft cloth to remove paint in various directions. For a soft colorwash technique that will not result in defined lines, cover a dry base coat with paint that you have diluted approximately 4 parts water to 1 part paint. Experiment and test, if desired, to get the result you wish (photo C).

Combing, stippling, dragging and flogging each require different tools but similar techniques. For combing (photo D), use a purchased tool with various-sized teeth spaced at various distances, or make your own comb from cardboard or plastic. Combing can produce stripes, plaids or checker-

D

E

boards when dragged in different directions over the wet glazed/painted surface. Tools labeled for stippling, dragging and flogging are available at home improvement or hardware stores. Packages include instructions on achieving desired effects.

Faux finishes are surfaces painted to resemble something else, such as marble, wood grain, stone, stained glass, rust, patina and terra-cotta. Many are a combination of the techniques above. Some use special paints; some, special tools such as a wood grain roller or rocker or a feather for veining marble.

To produce an aged finish, simply sand areas and edges to reveal the natural wood surface. You may also apply stain or shoe polish to the surface and rub off as much as you like to achieve the desired effect (photo E). Other methods for giving the illusion of age include using a stiff brush to spatter the surface with paint or hitting the surface with a metal tool for a distressed look. The aging technique of crackling—demonstrated in this chapter with the crackled box

project—makes use of a crackling medium or weathered wood medium.

To add detail to a surface, create a taped, stenciled or stamped design. Masking tape works well to design stripes, squares and triangles. For borders or lettering on walls or craft projects, use stencils (as shown in the gilded project in this chapter). For simple patterned or random designs,

try rubber stamps or sponge stamps. For trompe l'oeil—fooling the eye—designs, start with a freehand sketch or combine stamping or stenciling techniques with freehand.

When it comes to painting technique combinations, the sky's the limit!

Faux Stained Glass

*C*reate an atmosphere of light and color with your own design of faux stained glass. Rich jewel colors accent a strong black line to make a translucent design to accent any window.

TOOLS & MATERIALS

- Pencil or marker
- Drawing paper
- Glass cut to desired size and shape
- Masking tape
- Opaque paint marker
- Paintbrush
- Stained glass acrylic colors

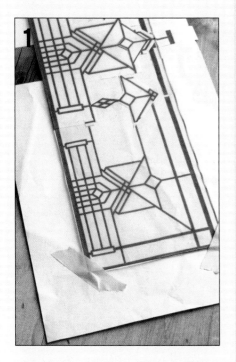

1 Using a pencil or marker, create your design on drawing paper. When placing the design, remember that the reverse side will be painted. Once all parts of the glass design are complete on paper, place them under a clean piece of glass. Tape down the four corners of the glass onto the design so the drawing does not shift during painting.

2 Using an opaque marker, carefully trace on the glass the paper design that is laid out underneath. To aid in tracing the design, turn the glass when moving from the top of the design to the bottom. Once the drawing has been transferred to the glass, remove the underlying paper design.

3 Stir acrylic color paints before using. Choose one color and determine all the areas you will fill in with this color. Dip paintbrush into the paint and drop the paint onto the glass surface.

To prevent streaking, use enough paint to cover an area with as few brush strokes as possible. To change coloring effect, a sponge can be used to mottle the paint as it is applied. Or, apply one color and with another brush, add a different color for a marbling effect. Allow to dry for several hours. Apply a clear acrylic spray to protect colors from fading.

Floral Floor Cloth

*Y*ou have art on your walls … now decorate the floor when you create this great custom floor cloth for a favorite space.

TOOLS & MATERIALS

- Paintbrushes (several sizes depending on your design)
- Acrylic (or latex) paints
- Pre-primed canvas
- Pencil
- Water-soluble polyurethane
- Straightedge ruler
- Scissors
- Tacky glue or contact cement

1 Paint canvas blue; let dry. Pencil in, and then paint, the flowers and leaves—painting several coats of each color for good coverage.

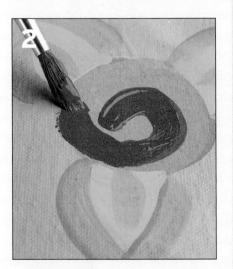

2 Paint the outlines. Paint the polka dots. Let dry overnight before hemming, and sealing with water-soluble polyurethane.

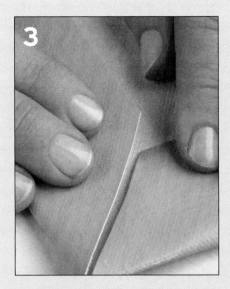

3 With a straightedge ruler, mark cutting lines around the floor cloth, allowing 1½ inches. Fold 1½ inches of canvas over on each side. Miter, or cut diagonally, each edge to remove the bulkiness of extra canvas. Glue with tacky glue or contact cement.

4 Using a bigger brush, coat the front of the floor cloth with water-soluble polyurethane two or three times, allowing it to dry completely between coats. Also add one coat of sealer to back of the floor cloth; dry completely. After it's dry, let it dry a few days before placing it on the floor.

5 Floor cloths can only be used on hard-surfaced interior floors such as wood or linoleum. Because floor cloths are sealed on the underside, they tend to be slippery on a wooden or linoleum floor. Cut rug-gripping material (sold at home stores in the carpeting area) to size and place it under the floor cloth to keep it in place.

$

*M*etal ceiling tiles make great mats for photos, giving them a fun antique look. Using metallic and matte paints, you can give the tile an aged patina appearance.

TOOLS & MATERIALS

- Ruler
- Photo
- Pencil
- Metal ceiling tile (12- by 12-inch)
- Utility knife
- Brown matte spray paint
- Paintbrushes:
  - No. 12 flat
  - No. 4 round
- Metallic acrylic paints:
  - Copper, Gold, Green Patina
- Empty spray bottle or spray attachment for acrylic paints
- Matte interior sealer
- Quik Dry Tacky Glue
- 3 (1-inch) mauve ribbon roses
- 3 (3/8-inch) pink ribbon roses
- Foam brush
- Wood frame (12- by 12-inch)
- 4 (3¾-inch) decorative Walnut Hollow wood trim
- Masking tape or clear packing tape

1 Measure size of picture and decrease by ½ inch on all sides. Using ruler and pencil, draw opening in center of metal ceiling tile. Using utility knife, cut out opening.

2 Spray metal ceiling tile with brown matte spray paint. Using flat brush, paint Copper over entire ceiling tile surface allowing some of the brown paint to show through. Using Green Patina in a spray bottle, randomly spritz ceiling tile. Using round brush, paint Gold accents on raised areas on tile. Using sealer, brush over entire metal ceiling tile. Glue ribbon roses in upper right corner of opening.

3 Using foam brush, paint frame and decorative wood trim pieces Copper. Glue one decorative wood trim piece to center of each side of the frame. Tape picture in place on back side of metal ceiling tile.

Pansies Cake Dome

This cake dome will delight all your guests, especially when you add real pansies to the delicacy that is under the dome! The trick to painting on glass with acrylic paints is to use frosted glass spray as a base coat.

TOOLS & MATERIALS

- Glass cake dome (6½- by 10-inch)
- Frosted glass spray
- Pansy flower pattern
- Tracing paper
- Scissors
- Transparent tape
- Pencil
- Paintbrushes:
    - No. 12 flat shader
    - No. 10/0 liner
    - No. 2 round
- Acrylic paints:
    - Dazzling Metallic Emperor's Gold, Green Mist, Hauser Dark Green, Olive Green, Peach Sherbet, Baby Pink, Moon Yellow, Wisteria, Gingerbread, Boysenberry, Yellow Ochre, Royal Purple, Hi-Lite Flesh, Pink Chiffon, Pineapple, Lilac, Lamp Black and Titanium White
- Stylus
- Rust-oleum

1 **For Dome:** Following manufacturer's directions, spray outside of glass cake dome with frost and allow to dry. Trace pattern onto tracing paper. Cut out pattern to fit inside cake dome lid. Place pattern inside lid and secure with transparent tape. Using pencil, lightly trace pattern onto lid. Evenly space pansy design and apply desired amount of flowers.

For Knob: Paint knob Dazzling Metallic Emperor's Gold.

For Leaves: Base-coat each leaf: Green Mist. Shade each leaf: Hauser Dark Green. Highlight each leaf: Olive Green.

For Bud: Base-coat each bud: Peach Sherbet, Baby Pink, Moon Yellow and Wisteria. Shade each bud: Gingerbread, Boysenberry, Yellow Ochre and Royal Purple. Highlight each bud: Hi-Lite Flesh, Pink, Pink

Chiffon, Pineapple and Lilac. Pulling liner brush through both Green Mist and Hauser Dark Green, add greenery around bud in Green Mist and Hauser Dark Green.

For Pansy: Follow bud-painting directions.

2 Using the liner brush, start in the center of the pansy and pull Lamp Black lines out through front petals.

3 Using round brush, tap in Moon Yellow. Shade lower edge of center Yellow Ochre, and lightly tap in highlight along upper edge with Pineapple. Using liner brush, add Titanium White comma strokes on each side of center.

4 Using stylus, randomly dot a cluster of three dots with Dazzling Metallic Emperor's Gold. To achieve a clear dome, seal with an acrylic varnish. If a frosted effect is to remain, seal only the flowers and buds with an acrylic varnish.

Gift Box with Stars

$ $

*T*his is an easy and attractive way to give a present to a special person. Not only is the box used to hold the gift, but then the recipient can use it to store treasured keepsakes in days to come.

TOOLS & MATERIALS

- 1-inch sponge brush
- Wood sealer
- Wood box (7- by 7- by ⅜-inch)
- Fine grit sandpaper
- Paper towels
- Acrylic paint:
    - Dazzling Metallic Emperor's Gold, Jade Green, Cranberry Wine and Light Mocha
- DecoArt Weathered Wood
- Paintbrushes:
    - No. 4 flat shader
    - No. 4 round
- 8 (1-inch) primitive stars
- 3 (1½-inch) primitive stars
- 3 (½-inch) adhesive foam mounts
- Wood glue
- Ruler
- Scissors
- 2 (12- by 12-inch) sheets scrapbook paper
- Quik Dry Tacky Glue
- Craft knife

1 Using sponge brush, apply wood sealer to the box. Let dry and sand lightly. Wipe off dust with paper towels. Using sponge brush, paint entire box Dazzling Metallic Emperor's Gold. Let dry. Following manufacturer's directions and using sponge brush, apply Weathered Wood over the entire box. Let dry. Using sponge brush, apply Jade Green over Weathered Wood being sure to follow manufacturer's directions. Using the sponge brush, paint the edge of the lid with 3 coats of Cranberry Wine.

2 Using No. 4 flat shader brush, paint all stars with Emperor's Dazzling Metallic Emperor's Gold; let dry. Following manufacturer's directions and using No. 4 flat shader brush, apply Weathered Wood over each star. Let dry. Using No. 4 flat shader brush, apply Light Mocha over Weathered Wood being sure to follow manufacturer's directions. Using adhesive foam mounts, mount 3 larger stars onto lid. Using wood glue, adhere 4 smaller stars to lid and 1 star to each side of box.

Dip the handle end of the No. 4 round brush into Cranberry Wine and randomly add dots around stars on lid.

3 Using No. 4 round brush, paint lid and base edges Dazzling Metallic Emperor's Gold. Measure all inside areas and cut scrapbook paper to fit. Glue in place. Use craft knife to trim edges extending beyond box edges.

Terra-Cotta Canister Set

$ $

This fruit-themed canister set will look great in any kitchen. Plus, the entire project is inexpensive and very easy to do! You can find terra-cotta flowerpots at any store carrying gardening supplies.

TOOLS & MATERIALS

- Terra-cotta flowerpots (1 each):
  - 7½ inches high by 8¾ inches wide
  - 5⅝ inches high by 6¾ inches wide
  - 4½ inches high by 5¼ inches wide
  - 4 inches high by 4½ inches wide
- Terra-cotta flowerpot drain dishes (1 each)
  - 8½ or 9½ inches wide
  - 7⅜ inches wide
  - 5¾ inches wide
  - 5 inches wide
- Snow White spray paint
- Low-tack painter's masking tape
- Paintbrushes:
  - No. 10 flat shader
  - No. 8 flat shader
  - No. 4 flat shader
  - No. 4 round
  - No. 5/0 liner

- Acrylic paints:
  - Lamp Black, Dazzling Metallic Emperor's Gold, Grape Juice, Dioxazine Purple, Wisteria, Arbor Green, Deep Teal, Green Mist, Light Cinnamon, Sable Brown, Raw Umber, Santa Red, Antique Maroon, Cadmium Red, Burnt Sienna, True Ochre, Terra-Cotta, Pineapple, Coral Rose, Buttermilk, White Wash
- Pencil
- Tracing paper
- Black graphite paper
- Fruit pattern
- Paper towels
- Sponge
- Feather (wing-type feather)
- Stylus
- Quick-drying glue
- 2 (1½-in.) knob-head balls
- 2 (1¼-in.) knob-head balls

1 **For Each Terra-Cotta Pot:** Spray each terra-cotta drain dish and pot Snow White; let dry completely.

Around lip edge, vertically place tape strips side by side. Remove every other tape strip. Using No. 10 flat shader brush, paint open areas Lamp Black. Remove remaining tape. Using No. 4 flat shader, paint Emperor's Gold stripes next to the Lamp Black stripes.

2

Brown. Using No. 8 flat shader brush, highlight opposite side and tip of stem Raw Umber.

For Apple: Using No. 5/0 liner brush, paint a small Santa Red stripe along right side of each Emperor's Gold stripe. Using No. 10 flat shader brush, base-coat with Santa Red. Using same brush, shade left side and top indentation Antique Maroon. Using No. 8 flat shader brush highlight right side and a small reflective area in Cadmium Red. Using No. 8 flat shader brush, shade bottom edge Burnt Sienna. Using No. 4 round brush, base-coat stem Light Cinnamon. Using No. 4 round brush, shade left side of stem Sable Brown. Using No. 4 round brush, highlight with Raw Umber on opposite side, as well as on tip of stem.

Using No. 8 flat brush, base-coat leaf Arbor Green. Using same brush, shade the lower edge and center vein Deep Teal. Using No. 4 flat shader brush, highlight upper edge and center vein Green Mist.

For Pear: Using No. 5/0 liner brush, paint a True Ochre stripe along right side of each Emperor's Gold stripe. Using No. 10 flat shader brush, base-coat pear True Ochre. Using No. 8 flat shader brush, shade the left side and top indentation Terra-Cotta. Using No. 8 flat shader brush, highlight right side, top indentation, and highlight stroke Pineapple. Using fabric brush, dip into Coral Rose.

Remove excess paint from brush onto paper towels before applying a blush area to lower center area on pear. Using No. 4 round brush, base-coat stem Light Cinnamon. Using No. 4 round brush, shade left side of stem Sable Brown. Using No. 4 round brush, highlight with Raw Umber on opposite side as well as on top of stem. Using No. 8 flat brush, base-coat leaf Arbor Green. Using No. 4 flat shader brush, shade upper edge and center vein Deep Teal. Using No. 4 flat brush, highlight lower edge and center vein Green Mist.

2 Using pencil and tracing paper, trace pattern. Slipping graphite paper between pot and traced pattern, retrace pattern onto terra-cotta pot.

For Grapes: Using No. 5/0 liner brush, paint a small Grape Juice stripe along right side of each Emperor's Gold stripe. Using No. 8 flat shader, paint grape areas Grape Juice. Using No. 8 flat shader, shade behind each grape Dioxazine Purple; with same brush, highlight on top of each grape Wisteria. Using No. 8 flat shader brush, base-coat leaf Arbor Green. Using same brush, shade the upper edge and center vein Deep Teal. Using No. 8 flat shader brush, highlight lower edge and center vein Green Mist. Using No. 4 round brush, base-coat stem Light Cinnamon. Using No. 8 flat shader brush, shade left side of stem Sable

3

For Lids: Using sponge, paint top of each lid Buttermilk and White Wash to give a faux effect. Drag feather through puddle of Emperor's Gold, then add vein lines to achieve a faux marble look. Using No. 8 flat brush, paint Lamp Black around the rim on top of the lid and Emperor's Gold to lower lip edge.

Using stylus, dip into Lamp Black and randomly add dots around edge of each dish. Glue knob heads in center of each lid. Using No. 10 flat brush, paint each knob head Emperor's Gold.

For Cherries: Using No. 5/0 liner brush, paint a Santa Red stripe along the Emperor's Gold stripe. Using No. 10 flat shader brush, base-coat each cherry Santa Red. Using No. 8 flat shader brush, shade the left side and indentation Antique Maroon. Using No. 8 flat shader brush, highlight right side and indentation. Using No. 4 flat shader brush, highlight stroke Cadmium Red. Using No. 4 round brush, base-coat stems Light Cinnamon. Using No. 5/0 liner brush, add a Sable Brown line on left side and Raw Umber on right side of each stem. Using No. 8 flat shader brush, base-coat each leaf Arbor Green. Using No. 4 flat shader brush, shade left edges on two leaves; one leaf on upper edge; and center vein Deep Teal. Using No. 4 flat brush, highlight lower edge and center vein Green Mist.

Gilded Charger

$

*A*dd sparkle and elegance to your table setting with this gilded charger. A charger adorns your table until dinner plates are in use. Tailor your design to your decor using a free-hand design, a traditional shape created from a template, or an overall gilded look.

TOOLS & MATERIALS

- Wooden charger
- Red latex paint
- Stencil
- Painter's masking tape
- 1-inch paintbrush
- Adhesive
- Cosmetic sponge
- Artist's brush (size depends on free-hand design)
- Copper metal leaf
- Scissors
- Tweezers
- Stencil brush
- Aerosol finish in semigloss

1 For a traditional gilded project, paint wooden charger with a red base coat; let dry. For the stenciled project, use a stain-finished charger. Determine the center placement of stencil, then tape it into place.

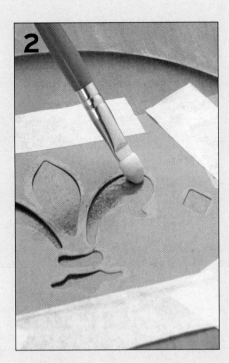

2 With 1-inch paintbrush, apply a thin layer of adhesive to gilded project. With cosmetic sponge, apply a thin layer of adhesive to stencil project, tapping it on. With artist's paintbrush, apply adhesive in thin layer with free-hand motion. Adhesive will appear milky until it is dry, about 60 minutes.

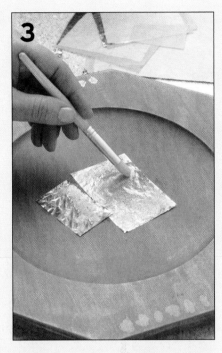

3 Try not to get fingerprints on the metal leaf. For stenciled project, remove stencil and then apply metal leaf, as follows, for all three projects: Pick up metal leaf, keeping the piece of paper covering it in place. Cut the metal leaf into pieces that are small enough to control and cover portions of the design area. Using tweezers, transfer metal leaf with paper, to project and tap metal leaf down with a stencil brush, adhering it. Continue covering design areas until covered as desired. Use small pieces to fill in areas, if needed. Gently brush the metal leaf surface to remove extra metal leaf and to give a brushed texture. Seal with acrylic spray or varnish.

Create the popular look of a painted quote on any wall. The kitchen is a great room, but so are kids' rooms and family rooms. This custom wallpaper banner is easy, inexpensive and you don't need to know calligraphy to do it. Choose your own font (letter style).

TOOLS & MATERIALS

- Quote
- Computer
- Printer
- Scissors
- Painter's tape
- Graphite paper
- Pencil
- Artist's paintbrush with fine tip
- 2 oz. acrylic paint

1 Select a quote and type it on your computer, using the underlining feature. Select a font that complements the quote, and enlarge it until it is the size that you'd like for your wall. Print the quote out, and tape the quote together into a long strip, using the underlining from word to word to keep it straight, with the same amount of space between each word. Cut away excess paper.

2 Using painter's tape, attach the quote on the wall, making sure it is level. Slip graphite paper under the quote, and with a pencil, carefully trace around the letters.

3 With a steady hand, paint in the letters, giving them a second coat if needed.

Sewing Decor and Crafts

In days gone by, sewing was a money-saving activity. Times have changed. Today, we sew or quilt for relaxation and creativity—to make crafts, home accents and fashion accessories.

Equipment and Tools

A recent model sewing machine will best handle contemporary fabrics such as knits and polar fleece. A good basic machine will serve you well. Keeping your sewing machine in good working order is important. If your machine hasn't been used for a long time or is a hand-me-down, bring it in for a tune-up.

If you get into decorative sewing, you might have fun with a machine that offers various embroidery features and programmable stitches. As an addition to your sewing equipment, you might also consider a serger, which will finish edges very quickly, make professional-looking rolled hems and more. For any type of sewing, you will definitely need a reliable, sturdy steam iron.

A good stitch requires the right tension. This means that when stitching, the top and bottom thread meet within the fabric's center (if you could view a cross section). If the top thread pulls to the bottom or the bottom thread pulls to the top, the tension needs adjusting. Check your machine's manual for specific instructions.

Common presser foot attachments include the zipper foot, for sewing next to piping; the special-purpose foot and zigzag plate for wide stitches like the zigzag stitch; the single-stitch foot and plate for use when you will only be straight stitching. For quilting, you might find yourself using a quilt guide, an even-feed or walking foot or a darning foot.

When it comes to needles, remember always to start a new project with a

Organize your sewing equipment and tools.

new needle in the machine, as dull needles can affect the stitch quality. Sewing machine needles come with various points and in various sizes and should be matched to the specific project. Use a sharp point with woven and nonwoven fabrics and a ballpoint with knit fabrics. A universal point will work with most fabrics. Use size 11 for fine fabrics, size 14 for medium-weight fabrics; and size 16 for heavy fabrics such as denim.

Thread comes in three basic weights. Extra-fine works well for machine embroidery and lightweight fabrics. Use all-purpose thread for general sewing. For decorating or heavy sewing, look for topstitching thread or buttonhole twist. You'll find cotton and cotton-wrapped thread for sewing on natural fibers such as cotton or wool and for most general sewing. Use polyester thread for sewing on synthetic fibers, such as polyester and nylon. Other threads are available, such as rayon for a sheen; metallic; nylon for nearly invisible stitching; variegated for colorful satin or decorative stitches; thread on a cone for the serger; and woolly nylon for stretch and for the rolled hem on the serger.

A fabric shears, with its bent handle, works best and is most comfortable for cutting fabric. Specialty shears for cutting knits and slippery fabrics are also available. For fine work, try embroidery scissors or sewing scissors (handles are equal). Never use your fabric shears on paper or any non-fabric material, as doing so will dull them. A seam ripper can prove invaluable, and you may also want to use a thread clipper.

If you're cutting fabric for quilting, crafts or home decorating, a rotary cutter and self-healing mat will make the job quick and easy. Safety is of utmost importance, as the rotary blade is very sharp; when it's not in use, close the safety lock. Rotary cutters and mats come in various sizes. If you take your projects on the road, a smaller mat will serve your portability needs. For quilting, a large mat will be most efficient along with a permanent cutting surface (if you have the option).

You'll find measuring tools to be as valuable as your cutting tools and sewing machine. Aside from your ruler and yardstick, the basics include a measuring tape, seam gauge for small measurements and a square. For use in conjunction with a rotary cutter and mat, you'll need a see-through grid ruler, preferably one with one metal edge. For quilting and most crafts, you'll use marking tools such as tailor's chalk, tailor's pencil, silver pencil (for quilting) or marking pens that either wash off or disappear within 48 hours.

Pins will help you hold fabrics as you go. Pins with plastic heads and ball points work well with all fabrics. When using a rotary cutter and mat, you may choose to hold fabrics in place with weights (not shown). Sharps—all-purpose hand-sewing needles—are handy to have; get a package with various sizes. Certain projects may also require specialty hand-sewing needles. Other helpful notions include a needle threader, a thimble and a traditional, wrist or magnetic pincushion.

Manufacturers continually offer helpful new products for sewing and quilting, so browse through your craft or fabric store regularly. You might like using temporary spray adhesive for pattern placement or temporary appliqué placement. For design transfers, you have several options. You can purchase fabric sheets for use in a printer onto which you can print digital photos, scanned designs or original designs from a computer. Or you can use iron-on transfer paper in a photocopier to copy designs or photos, then transfer them to fabric, quilt blocks, T-shirts or tote bags.

Personalize your craft using favorite photos and iron-on paper.

31

Fabrics vary greatly—from sheers and lace to heavyweight.

You may choose fashion fabrics for home decorating projects. Denim can make a great pillow or duvet cover. Polar fleece has been popular for throws, pillows and even curtains. (Polar fleece edges do not fray so they don't need finishing; however, when you're stitching polar fleece, be sure to hold it taut to avoid feeding layers unevenly.)

For quilting, medium-weight cottons or cotton-blends are typically used. Some quilt projects are made from wool or flannel or with a flannel backing. All types of fabrics are available in large ranges of colors and prints. For fashion accessories, fabrics are usually heavier and may be home decorating or upholstery fabrics. For craft projects, a variety of fabric types may be used, including fur, chenille, polar fleece, denim and home decorating fabrics.

Used between two layers of fabric, fusible or sew-in interfacing offers support or stabilization. Sew-in interfacing is not commonly used in crafting and home decorating projects as fusible interfacing is much easier to use. Sheets of paper-backed fusible web work well for appliqué projects. You can fuse the web to the fabric, draw and cut the design, remove the paper, then fuse the fabric shape to the project. Non-woven or knit fusible web in narrow strips works well for fusing edges and seams.

Fabrics

Lightweight fabrics include sheeting. Medium-weight fabrics include chintz, usually with a shiny surface; sateen, a bit heavier with a subtle sheen; moiré or damask, both with subtle woven designs; linen, duck or lightweight canvas woven with a flat finish. Novelty weaves are also available and offer rich texture options. In most fabric stores, you'll likely find a section stocked with home decorating fabrics in a selection of colors, prints, designs and weights.

For table items or items you don't want to have to dry clean, be sure to check whether the fabric is washable.

At fabric stores, you'll also find various trims and tassels and other notions such a grommets, café curtain rings, zippers and hook-and-loop tape. For some decorating projects, you'll also need hardware such as curtain rods, shower curtain rods and hooks, and tieback hooks. Most of these are available in larger fabric and craft stores.

Tips and Techniques

When you're sewing for crafts and home decorating, you will not use the ⅝-inch seams traditionally used in clothing construction. Most seams in home decorating sewing projects will be ½ inch. Quilting projects use ¼-inch seams. Seams for craft projects vary (so check instructions carefully). If you are using a woven fabric that will fray, be sure to finish all seams. For example, with a sheer fabric for curtains, you

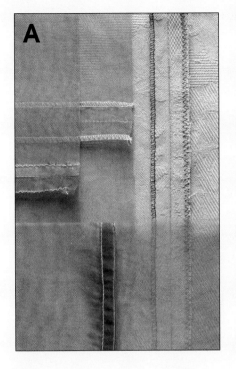

A

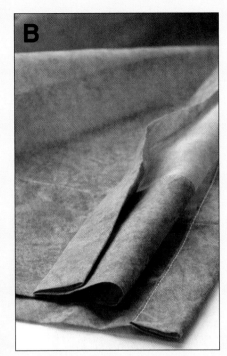

B

C

may finish seams with a zigzag stitch along the edge; a French seam; or a serged edge or serged seam. For a medium- or heavyweight fabric, finish the seams by zigzagging or serging (photo A).

Side hems on curtains, tablecloths, placemats or napkins are usually a double fold ½- or 1-inch hem. Bottom

hems on long curtain panels tend to be wider, up to 3 inches. To stitch a hem, machine stitch along its edge (photo B). Curtains often require casings or rod pockets at the tops. To create a casing or rod pocket, make a ½-inch fold, then enough of a fold to accommodate the rod depth plus stitching; stitch along the edge. If you want a header or ruffle above the rod pocket (shown), take this

into account when measuring and folding (photo C).

Key fabric terms to know include selvage, crosswise grain, straight grain and bias. Selvage edges are the uncut edges of a piece of purchased fabric. The crosswise grain runs from selvage to selvage. The straight, or lengthwise, grain runs at a 90-degree angle to the crosswise grain. The bias runs at a 45-degree angle to the crosswise grain. You can cut your own bias strips to use for binding or for decorative piping. You can also purchase binding or piping in various colors. Making your own bias strips allows you to customize your project with coordinating fabric. To make bias strips, cut fabric to the desired width along the bias grain. Trim off selvages and seam strips together (photo D). Because bias stretches, it works well around curves and corners. To make piping, enclose cording in the center of bias strips and use the zipper foot to stitch close to the cording (photo E).

D

E

Patchwork Tab Curtain

$ $

This fun, easy patchwork tab top curtain is hung by fabric loops from your favorite decorative curtain rod. It's hard to predict what you will enjoy more—creating this fun and easy patchwork tab curtain … or sitting back and enjoying the look it brings to any room.

TOOLS & MATERIALS

- Brown paper
- Scissors
- Pencil
- Ruler
- Pen for marking fabric

- 4 or 5 different cotton fabrics, amounts depend on size of valance
- Matching thread
- Sewing machine
- Pins
- Curtain rod

1 Cut a piece of brown paper the finished size of the valance. Using a pencil and ruler, draw rectangles or squares on the paper. Cut out shapes, lay on fabric and, using a pen and ruler, mark a ¼-inch seam allowance around entire piece. Cut out the fabric on the marked line. Sew fabric pieces together to form blocks. Sew blocks together using a ¼-inch seam allowance to form your fabric.

2 Install curtain rod high enough so that the upper edge of the valance covers the window frame. The valance length, not including the tabs, can be determined by taping up different lengths of paper valances. The width of the valance should be approximately twice the width of the window frame.

To determine the tab length and width, pin fabric strips over the curtain rod. Using pins, mark tabs at desired distance from rod. Add ¼ inch to length for seam allowance. The width of the tab should be two times the desired width plus ½ inch for seam allowance. Determine the number of tabs needed by placing one tab on each end of the valance and spacing the remaining tabs 5 to 7 inches apart.

3 Fold each tab in half lengthwise with right sides together. Stitch down the long edge using a ¼-inch seam allowance. Turn tab right side out. Center the seam on back of each tab and press. Fold tab in half and pin to top edge of valance at markings. Match raw edges and baste in place.

4 Cut lining the same length and width as valance. Pin to front of valance with right sides together. Stitch using a ¼-inch seam around all sides, leaving a 10-inch opening at bottom. Clip corners; turn right side out and slipstitch opening closed. Press well and slip loops onto rod and hang.

Heirloom Guest Towel

This delicate linen guest towel, edged with elegant beading and delicate lace, makes a beautiful accessory for any powder room.

TOOLS & MATERIALS

- Linen guest towel (14 by 21 inches)
- Scissors
- ½ yard of ½-inch beading lace
- ½ yard of 1¼-inch edging lace
- Sewing machine
- Sewing machine needles (size 70)
- 50- or 80-weight fine cotton thread

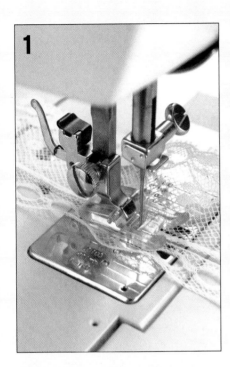

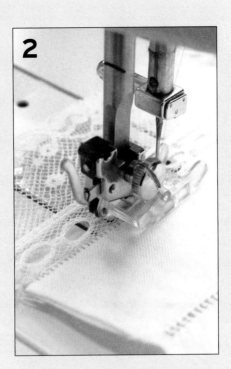

1 Measure the width of the guest towel and cut beading lace and edging lace 2 inches longer. Place strips of lace side by side, with right side of laces up. Match the pattern of the laces if they are similar. Butt the two laces together so that the edges meet, but do not overlap. Set your sewing machine on zigzag and select a stitch width that is wide enough to catch the two headings on the pieces of lace. Stitch length should be short, but not tight. Start sewing ¼ inch from the edge of the pieces to be joined. This makes it easier for the sewing machine to feed the laces.

2 Join the created lace trim to one end of the towel. Extend lace trim 1 inch on either side of the towel. With right sides up, butt the laces and fabric edge up together so that the edges meet, but do not overlap. With a narrow zigzag and a short stitch length, sew lace to fabric edge with half of the zigzag stitch going onto the fabric and the other half on the edge of the lace.

3 To hem the ends of the lace, turn back the 1-inch extension to the wrong side, zigzag close to the edge of the lace. Trim excess fabric away from sewn edge.

Pieced and Quilted Pillow Top

*T*his is an easy and rewarding first quilting project. Make this pillow even easier when you simply tie or sew buttons at the intersections, instead of quilting. Instructions are for a 24-inch pillow, but you can make it larger or smaller by increasing or decreasing the number of squares.

TOOLS & MATERIALS

- Quilter's 45-inch-width flannel: back of pillows and squares – 30 inches; 5 pieces of 6-inch fabric (choose 2 solids, 2 plaid and 2 prints)
- Shears or rotary cutter and mat
- See-through ruler
- Thread
- Hand-sewing needle
- Pins

- Iron
- 25-inch square muslin or broadcloth (for backing of pieced pillow top)
- 25-inch square cotton batting
- Safety pins
- Sewing machine
- Marking pencil
- 24-inch square pillow form

1 Square up the fabric pieces before cutting, by stretching in the direction needed to make it square. Cut a 24½-inch square from: fabric for the pillow back, muslin and batting; set aside. Cut 4½-inch strips from each fabric. Cut 4½-inch squares from plaid individually. Stack the other fabric strips on top of one another, lining up edges, and cut into 6 (4½- by 4½-inch) squares. Lay out squares to determine their placement and stack rows in order.

Stitch squares together into a row of 6 squares, using a ¼-inch seam allowance. Secure seams, beginning and end, by backstitching. Repeat for 5 more rows. Press seams open. Pin rows together, two at a time, matching seams. Stitch rows together using a ¼-inch seam allowance. Press seams open.

2 Layer smoothly, from bottom up as follows: Muslin, batting, and pieced top, right side up. Pin baste at each seam intersection with safety pins. Stitch from the center out and then stitch each quarter quadrant. Stitch-in-the-ditch, letting machine stitching fall into the seam indentation, so that it is barely visible (contrast thread was used for photograph). Hold fabrics taut when stitching to prevent puckering. Do not secure seams by backstitching. When finished stitching, leave a 2-inch length of top and bobbin thread, then cut. Pull top thread to the back and tie.

3 Determine which squares to channel quilt. This project has the solid colored squares quilted. Mark each square to be quilted, at 1-inch intervals. Alternate the direction of stitching lines, for more interest. Using matching thread (contrast thread was used for photograph), secure beginning and end by pulling top thread through to bottom and tying in a knot; this can be done after all stitching is complete. Square up the pillow top, if there was any stretching.

To make pillow cover, place pillow back and top, right sides together. Trim all sides even and square. Stitch around three sides with ½-inch seam allowance, as determined by the fit desired with the pillow form. On the last side, stitch 4 inches in from each corner. Press raw edges under ½ inch. Turn pillow cover right side out and put pillow form into pillow top. Turn at pressed edge and stitch closed by hand, with a slipstitch.

Appliqué Table Runner

*B*looming frayed-edged flowers make this gorgeous runner a real conversation piece. This project is easier than traditional appliqué, and even a sewing novice can do it. But sewing "pros" will have fun too.

TOOLS & MATERIALS

- Paper
- Pencil
- Ruler
- Dollar coin for making pattern
- Scissors
- Fabric marker
- ⅛ yard each of 3- to 6-inch cotton (not tightly woven) fabrics in prints or subtle plaids and 1 in green for leaves
- ½ yard paper-backed fusible web
- 1 yard (45 inches wide) home deco fabric for runner
- 1 yard (45 inches wide) home deco fabric for lining
- Iron
- Sewing machine
- Thread to blend with print of fabrics
- Thread to match bias tape
- 2 packages (½ inch) double fold bias tape
- Pins

15 by 34 inches. Cut 2 (22-inch-long) pieces. Zigzag all edges. Set aside the lining fabric.

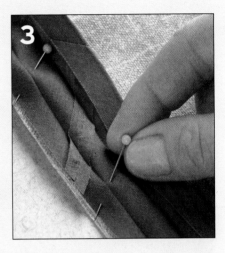

1 Make 4-inch flower pattern with 6 petals: On paper, trace a 3-inch circle and trace 6 smaller half-circles using a dollar coin around large circle. Make 4-inch leaf pattern. Cut out patterns. Make another set of patterns ⅛ inch smaller. Trace and cut 22 flowers from the print and plaid fabrics. From paper-backed web, trace, and cut 22 flowers from the reduced-size flower pattern. Leave paper on web and trace on paper side. Do the same for 8 leaves.

Square up the runner and lining fabrics, then cut two rectangles from each fabric, 15 inches wide and from selvage to selvage. Cut off selvages. On the main fabric, leave one rectangle 44 inches and cut the other into 2 (15-inch-long) pieces. Keep pieces going the same direction as the larger piece. At one end of each piece, trace a circle and cut. It should have a 7½-inch radius. For lining fabric, cut one large rectangle

2 Leaving paper on web, fuse web to back of flowers and leaves, by pressing, not ironing, according to manufacturer's directions. Find the center of the large rectangle and, using 10 flowers, create a circle. Keep flowers 1½ inches from edges of runner. Add 2 leaves to each side of the circle. When satisfied with design, peel off paper and fuse to runner. For ends of runner, find the center of half-circle and do as above, using 6 flowers to create a half-circle. Fuse. Do the same for other end of runner.

3 Using a sewing machine set on a narrow zigzag stitch, stitch around the flowers, ⅛ inch in from edges.

Sew rectangles together, pressing seams open. Sew seams in a similar manner on the lining fabric. Place fabric's wrong sides together, lining up edges, and cut the ends of the lining following the circular ends of runner.

Steam-shrink bias tape by ironing it with a hot-steam iron. Seam bias tape from each package together with ½-inch seam allowance and press open. To sew bias tape to runner, pin narrow edge of tape to top of runner, lining up edges. Starting ½ inch from the end, stitch along fold. Do not stretch bias. Before reaching the start of bias, fold it back, overlapping with end of the edges of the appliqué to make them fray a bit.

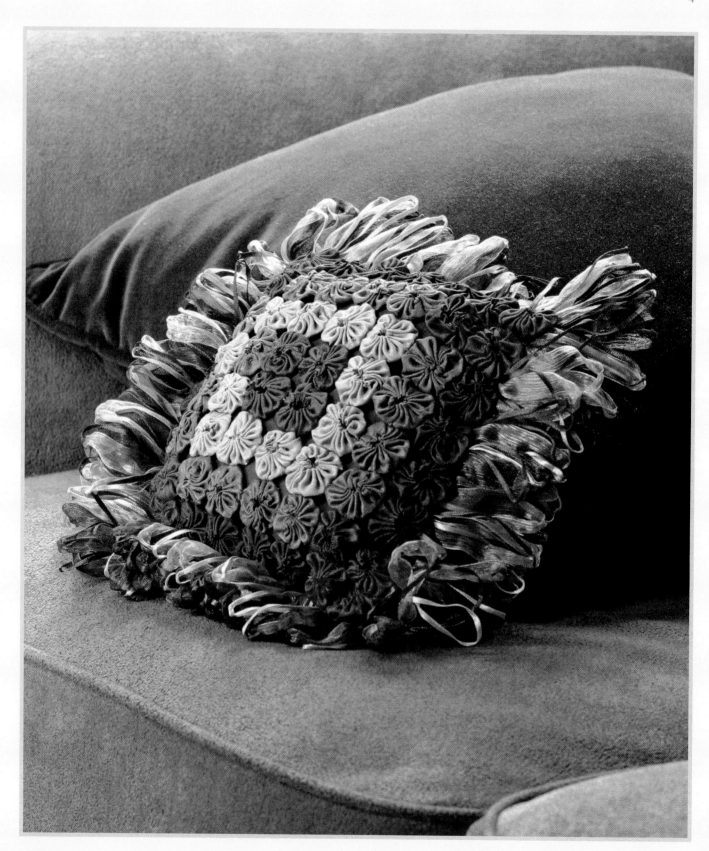

*I*n the 1920s through the 1940s, a popular craft was making "yo-yos" out of small scraps of calico and leftover fabrics, then using the little flowerettes in quilts and pillows. This project provides an elegant twist on that very old craft.

TOOLS & MATERIALS

- Cardboard
- Pencil or chalk
- 4 (⅓ yard each) fabrics of various colors
- Scissors
- Needle/thread
- Iron
- ½ yard of fabric to make pillow
- Pins
- Sewing machine
- Polyester fiberfill

1 Make a 4-inch cardboard circle template for fabric circles.

2 Using template, mark the circle on the back side of the fabric. Then, cut out the circles. You can cut several layers at once.

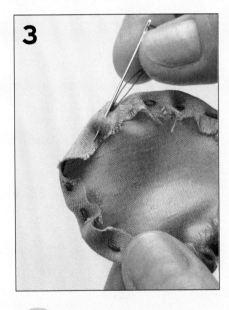

3 Thread a needle and knot the thread. With the wrong side of the fabric facing you, turn over approximately ¼-inch seam allowance like a hem and baste it with a running stitch all around the circle.

4 Once you have sewn the full circle, gently pull on the end of the thread to gather the edges of the yo-yo. Gather edges until center is just a small circle opening. Use your fingers to flatten circle and finger press the edges. Make a knot and pull needle through the middle of the yo-yo out through the side of the yo-yo. Cut the thread.

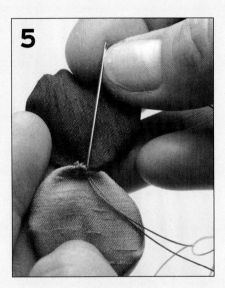

5 Put two yo-yos right sides together. With knotted thread, sew two or three stitches at the edge of both yo-yos. Make a knot. Run needle through the yo-yo and out through the side. Cut thread. Iron yo-yo square as flat as possible.

Once you have made and sewn the yo-yos together for the pillow (which determines the size of your pillow), measure the completed square. Cut two pieces of plain fabric in a square ⅝ inch larger than the measurement of the yo-yo square. Ruffle or trim is optional: If you are adding trim, pin the trim along the inside edges of the pillow square on the right side of the fabric, facing the trim towards the middle of the square. Sew around all the edges. Place the other pillow square on top of the trimmed square, right sides together, sewing a ⅝-inch seam. Backstitch at the beginning and ending of the stitching, leaving an opening of approximately 4 inches to add the polyester fiberfill. Turn right side out. Fill the pillow with fiberfill. Sew the opening of the pillow closed.

6 Lay the yo-yo square on top of the completed pillow. Pin it down to the center and corners of the pillow. Knot the thread and with a running stitch, sew the outside yo-yos at their seams all around the pillow. Remove the pins.

$ $

This cozy throw can decorate a garden bench or couch and warm you up on a cool evening. Tuck your feet into the pocket for toasty toes... or... slip the throw into the pocket for a soft pillow.

TOOLS & MATERIALS

- Fleece fabric (60 by 80 inches)
- Cutting board
- Sharp sewing scissors
- Sewing pins
- Yarn darner
- One skein yarn for edging

1 Place fleece on cutting board. Cut 20 inches off the 80-inch measure to make a throw size of 60 by 60 inches. Trim off any rough or uneven edges. From the excess fabric, cut a piece 20 by 22 inches. This will be used as the pillow pocket. Extra fabric can be used for additional pockets on the throw.

2 Spread throw fabric out on cutting board. On the lower edge, mark the center point of the fabric. Place cut fabric pocket center on this point with the 22-inch width at the top. Fold top edge of pocket under 1 inch. Pin down the fold and position the pocket on the center of the throw. Thread the yarn darner and knot the yarn at one end. Starting from the folded top of the pocket, blanket stitch the fold through pocket material only. To blanket stitch, enter the needle ½ inch from fabric edge on the wrong side of the fabric. Draw through hole and stitch down to bottom of edge. Enter again from wrong side of fabric, stitch down and catch last loop, bringing needle under and around to form a scalloped edge. Repeat to the end of the folded top of the pocket. Tie off and knot yarn ends. Stitch the two sides of the pocket to the throw sewing through both pieces of fabric.

3 Blanket stitch all four edges of the throw, stitching through the lower edge of the pocket as you go along the pocket edge. Lay completed stitched throw on flat surface. Turn fabric edges in lengthwise on two sides of the throw, folding underneath the pillow pocket. Next fold down from top edge to top of pocket. Slip throw fabric into the pocket, smoothing away bumps and creases. Extra fabric can be used to add additional pockets as part of the throw.

Sophisticated Tote

*M*ake an elegant but practical tote from tapestry, upholstery or drapery fabric. Line it in a medium-weight, durable fabric with enough pockets to satisfy your needs.

TOOLS & MATERIALS

- Shears or rotary cutter and mat
- ½ yard of medium-weight upholstery, tapestry or drapery fabric
- ½ yard lining fabric (medium-weight denim-type fabric or lightweight home decorating fabric)
- Plastic canvas (12½ by 4½ inches)

- Pins
- Sewing machine
- Matching thread
- Iron
- Pen for marking fabric
- Ruler

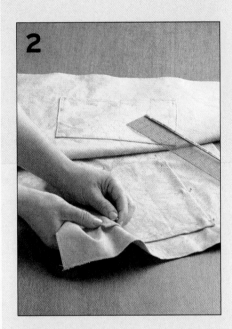

1 Cut 1 (30- by 18-inch) piece from the main fabric, and 2 (26- by 3½-inch) pieces from the lining fabric. Cut 1 (29- by 17½-inch) piece, 1(9- by 9-inch) piece and 1 (9- by 7-inch) piece from the lining fabric. Cut 1 (12- by 4½-inch) piece from the plastic canvas.

Fold main fabric piece in half cross-wise with right sides together; pin sides. Stitch each side using a ½-inch seam allowance. Secure beginning and ending of stitching by backstitching. Press seam open. Press bottom fold to mark and open corner, matching the seam and bottom fold. Pin. Mark a 4-inch line perpendicular to the seam. Stitch. Repeat for other side. Fold from corner to top of bag. Measure from center seam to folded edge to make sure the distance is equal. Pin and

stitch ⅛ inch from edge. Repeat for all sides of bag. Press ½ inch down around the top of bag. Insert plastic canvas.

2 Fold and press ½ inch around both pockets. Stitch top side of larger pocket, using ⅜-inch allowance. Center pocket, 2 inches from the top of the lining, and pin. Stitch around remaining sides of pocket. Add additional stitching lines to create more pockets. For smaller pocket, fold as above, and stitch one of the long edges for the top. Center 3 inches from top, pin, and stitch around remaining sides. Add additional stitching lines to create more pockets. Finish lining as above except for stitching the sides. Trim the points off the corners. Fold ½ inch down, around top edge of lining.

3 For Handles: Fold and press 1 inch along edge. Along other edge, fold and press ½ inch in. Fold, bringing folded edges even and pin. Stitch along folded edges and also along other edge. Put lining into bag. Pin, matching at seam. Continue to pin edge, keeping the lining edge a bit below the bag edge. Find the center of the front and back of bag. Measure either 2 or 2½ inches from center, insert handle, and pin. Repeat for both handles. Continue to pin lining to bag. Stitch around top, catching the lining.

Needle Arts

Needlepoint is the art of forming stitches on a special weave canvas.

Needlepoint

The obvious, precisely spaced holes in the canvas result in consistent stitches that conform to the canvas grid. The easiest way to do needlepoint is to work from a kit, which will contain everything you need, including the exact amount of yarn. A wide variety of needlepoint kits are available. For more creativity and to feel comfortable with all aspects of needlepoint, you may wish to design your own projects.

Canvas, a needlepoint project's typical base, is made either from cotton or a synthetic such as nylon. It is sized by gauge: Lower-gauge canvas with large holes is under 10 gauge; medium is 10 to 14 gauge; fine (with small holes) ranges from 16 to 20 gauge. The project design will determine the size canvas to use. Lower-gauge canvas is for designs with simple shapes and masses of color. Designs with lots of curves, shading and detail require fine-gauge canvas. Generally, the finer the canvas gauge, the more intricate the design and the longer the project will take. A needlepoint base may be a plastic grid rather than canvas. Plastic can lend more stiffness or even give structure to a project.

In kits, the design is stamped or painted on the canvas. Painted canvases, although costing more than stamped canvases, tend to be easier to follow. Another way to work needlepoint is to follow a chart of a design, translating it to the canvas as you work.

Needlepoint yarns—usually thicker than embroidery floss but not as thick as knitting yarns—are made of wool, cotton, silk, acrylic, rayon and even metallics. Traditionally and most com-

Coordinate the yarn color with the preprinted design.

monly used, wool offers durability for designs worked on items such as chair seat covers, glasses cases or purses. The yarn weight used for a project depends

Your local craft store stocks a variety of needlepoint yarns.

on the canvas gauge and sometimes the design. For lower-gauge canvas (which has large holes), you will use thick yarn such as Persian or rug yarn. For higher-gauge canvas (which has small holes), you may use embroidery floss. Various yarns and threads are sometimes used in one pattern for depth and detail.

When purchasing yarn for a needlepoint project, pay attention to the yarn's strand and ply. For example, each length of Persian yarn (2-ply, 3-strand) consists of 3 strands made from 2 threads each. Sometimes patterns call for yarn to be separated, using 1 or 2 strands of yarn to achieve the right thickness. Persian yarn and tapestry yarn are generally available only in needlework shops or online.

To work needlepoint, you will use a tapestry needle, which has a large eye and a blunt point that prevents the needle from piercing the canvas. Tapestry needles range from size 13 (the heaviest) to size 26 (the finest). The project's canvas gauge will determine the size needle to use; the finer the canvas gauge, the finer the needle. Check to see that the needle goes through the holes without distorting them. The most common size needle, No. 18, works well with the most commonly used canvas, 10- to 12-gauge.

Other tools used in needlepoint work include masking tape for binding the raw canvas edges, shears to cut canvas, embroidery scissors for fine work, a needle threader and a tape measure. To block the finished piece, you'll need a blocking board and tacks. A magnifier to reduce eyestrain is nice to have, as is a frame or hoop for holding the canvas as you work. Working in good light is essential. If you will create your own designs, you'll also need transfer tools, like transfer paper and pencil or water-soluble pens.

NEEDLEPOINT YARN CHARACTERISTICS

Persian yarn	2-ply, 3-strand yarn
Tapestry yarn	4-ply, single-strand yarn, also available in finer weights
Rug yarn	very thick 3-ply, single-strand yarn
Crewel yarn	fine 2-ply, single-strand yarn
Embroidery floss	multiple-strand thread
Pearl cotton	2-ply, single-strand thread
Metallic thread	available in various weights and textures, not very durable; used in small design areas

Basic Stitches

Like embroidery or knitting, needle-point consists of various types of stitches. You will be able to accomplish most needlepoint projects if you know the basic stitches, which include: half–cross stitch done horizontally (Illus. A); half–cross stitch done verti-cally (Illus. B); continental stitch done horizontally (Illus. C), continental stitch done vertically (Illus. D); and basketweave stitch (Illus. E and F).

To start stitching, leave 1 to 2 inches of yarn at the back of the canvas. Trap the yarn end with the first few stitches; trim off excess. On the masking tape binding (used to prevent canvas edges from fraying), label the top of the can-vas to ensure you continue working your stitches consistently. For some stitches, including the continental stitch, the canvas is turned a half turn, for each new row. To end stitching, bring the needle and yarn to the back of the canvas; weave yarn through the back side of the last few stitches and trim off excess.

Ribbon Embroidery

To work ribbon embroidery is simply to work embroidery stitches with rib-bon rather than with thread. Ribbon embroidery is often used to embellish fabric picture frames or boxes, pillows, clothing, greeting cards and more. The ribbon width raises the stitches, giving the project more texture. Silk ribbon in widths from 4 to 7 millimeters (mm) is most commonly used for embroidery, or you may choose synthetic ribbon in polyester or rayon. (Stiffer synthetic ribbons require designs worked in larger stitches.)

Using a wide range of colors can result in almost lifelike work; many ribbon embroidery designs create the look and feel of real flowers or leaves. Hand-dyed and variegated silk ribbon add elegance and interest to any design, and light and airy

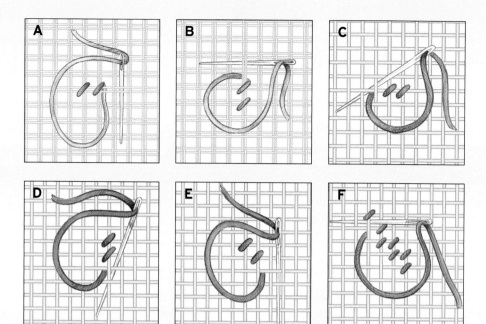

Create a look of depth and complexity combining ribbon with embroidery floss, metallic threads and even beads.

50

organdy ribbon contrasts nicely with silk ribbon.

To work ribbon embroidery, you'll use chenille needles and embroidery needles (also known as crewel needles). Chenille needles have a long eye and a sharp point. For 4- to 7-millimeter ribbon, size 18 is most common. In order to match the size to the floss, it will be helpful for you to have a packet of crewel needles in assorted sizes. You may also find a large tapestry needle handy to help tweak and shape ribbon as you work.

The fabric on which you add a ribbon embroidery design should be a medium weave that doesn't need a lot of ironing. Good fabrics to use include cotton, voile, shantung silk, faille, linen, moiré, satin and embroidery fabric such as aida and hardanger. As an exception, you may find a piece of velvet or wool that will make a beautiful project. If the fabric or garment will be washed, first wash the ribbon to ensure it is colorfast.

Transfer designs using water-soluble pens or fade-away pens, if you plan on finishing your project in a day, or with transfer pencil and tracing paper for more permanent marks. (Using a light box is helpful for this task.) Preprinted or iron-on traditional embroidery patterns work, but usually with ribbon embroidery a more sparse design is used, with design additions added or embellished as you go. Some designers just use a few marks to indicate flower placement and fill in the details while stitching.

It is best to work using an embroidery hoop. To prevent the embroidery from getting crushed, remove the hoop when you're not working on the project.

When working with ribbon, use a 12- to 16-inch length and take care not to let the ribbon twist. To begin stitching, thread the ribbon into the needle, then pierce the just-threaded end of the ribbon about ¼ inch from the end. Pull

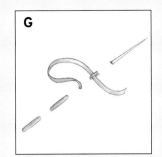

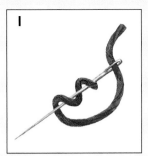

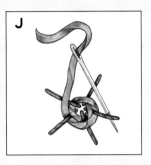

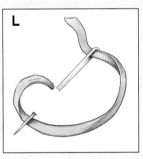

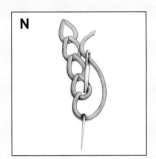

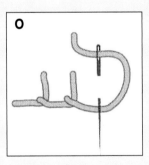

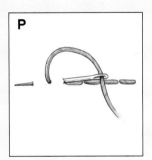

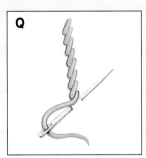

the long end of the ribbon to lock it firmly in place. Unlike regular embroidery, you should knot the ribbon end so that it doesn't pull through the fabric. Avoid pulling your stitches too tight. As you go, continually adjust the ribbon so its full width is visible on the top side of each stitch.

The most commonly used stitches include: Running stitch (Illus. G), French knots (Illus. H and I), Spider's web rose (Illus. J and K), Lazy daisy or detached chain (Illus. L and M), Chain stitch (Illus. N), Blanket stitch (Illus.

O), Backstitch (Illus. P) and Stem stitch (Illus. Q). Projects in this chapter use many of these stitches.

If you combine the above stitches with free-style stitches, you can create or duplicate an entire flower garden! You will find many projects to embellish with ribbon embroidery for you and others to admire.

*J*ournaling has become very popular among people of all ages. This wonderful journal would make the perfect gift for that special writer in your life. They can use it for poems, as a diary, for stories and memories … the possibilities are endless.

TOOLS & MATERIALS

- Ruler
- 45mm rotary cutter
- Cutting mat (12- by 18-inch)
- Black felt sheet
- Lightweight fusible interfacing
- 1 sheet of paper (the Paper Company: Metallic Gunmetal)
- Fine line permanent black marker
- Iron
- No. 10 embroidery needle
- White sewing thread
- Bucilla 100% Pure Silk Ribbon:
  - White No. 003, Periwinkle No. 574, Light Emerald No. 642
- No. 20 chenille needle
- 1 package White Opaque Seed Beads
- Super Tape (½-inch double-sided, acid-free bond)
- Linen sketch book (5¼- by 8¼-inch)

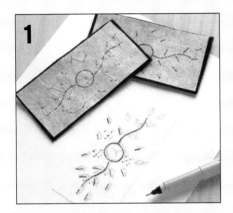

1 Cut a piece of black felt and interfacing 2 by 4 inches. Trim interfacing 1/16 inch on one vertical and horizontal side. Cut a piece of the Metallic Gunmetal paper 2½ by 4 inches. Set aside.

Using the black marker, trace the pattern onto the fusible side of interfacing. Iron interfacing to back side of felt. Using an embroidery needle and white sewing thread, baste along traced pattern lines. Baste rose circle and stitch the length of each lazy daisy; do not baste beads.

2 Silk ribbon basics: Pull long end until ribbon slides into place next to eye of the needle, making a knot. To begin stitching, leave a loose piece on the back side of the fabric, catch the loose ribbon with the needle after the first stitch, and pull the needle through the loose piece of silk to secure. To end the ribbon, tie it

off on the back side. Using the embroidery needle and white sewing thread, sew 5 even spokes in the circle for the spider's web rose base. Come up from the back side at the circle edge and down in center for each spoke. Use white silk ribbon and chenille needle to weave over and under the base threads. Come up from the back and weave around the spokes, pulling the first stitch so it covers the center of the base threads. When base threads are covered, end by tucking ribbon under the last row of the rose, pulling it to the back side to secure.

3 Use the green silk to work the stem stitch along the traced vine line. Come up from the back side at 1, keeping the thread on the lower side of the needle, going down at 2. Come up at 3, halfway between 1 and 2.

Use the green silk to work the lazy

daisy leaves along the vine. Come up from the back side at 1, allowing thread to lie on top of the fabric, forming a loop. Holding loop in place, go down at 2 right next (no space between) to 1. Bring needle up at 3 crossing over the thread, going down at 4. Repeat for each leaf.

Use the purple silk to work the detached lazy daises in the same manner as the leaves.

4 Use the white sewing thread to attach groups of beads. Sew through the bead twice to secure. Place beads nestled in among leaves.

5 Tape metallic paper to the front, upper-right corner, leaving approximately 1/8 inch between paper, top and right-side edge of journal. Center stitched felt piece in center of metallic paper, then tape in place.

Needlepoint Glass Case

*Y*arn scraps in a rainbow of vivid colors combine to create this great storage case. You'll also utilize blanket plastic canvas and a sampling of textural needlepoint stitches.

TOOLS & MATERIALS

- Ruler
- Scissors
- 7-mesh plastic canvas
- 7-mesh plastic canvas needle

- Yarn
- 4-ply plastic canvas yarn scraps in a variety of colors

1 Measure and cut two 3½- by 6¾-inch pieces from plastic canvas, cutting so the edges are smooth.

2 Thread the needle with the desired color of yarn. Using the stitch diagrams as guides, cover one canvas (front of case) with rows of stitches. You can use traditional needlepoint stitches on the entire piece, or use a variety of stitches. Do not use extremely long stitches or the yarn will have a tendency to snag.

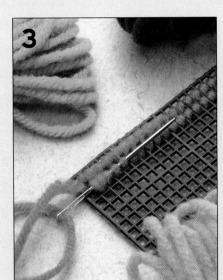

3 To end a color or change colors, run the needle through a few stitches on the back side to secure. Trim the tails.

4 For the back of the case, cover the canvas in simple needlepoint stitches, using one color if desired.

5 When both pieces are completely stitched, determine which two short sides will be used for the opening in the case. Choose one color of yarn and whipstitch the ends.

6 Align the stitched front and back, wrong sides together. Whipstitch the two long sides and bottom together, going through both layers. Secure the end of the yarn under a few stitches on the inside of the case; clip the tail.

Duplicate Stitch Sweater

Choose all your favorite colors to accent a solid color sweater for a one-of-a-kind look that is totally you!

TOOLS & MATERIALS

- Solid-color cotton turtleneck sweater with a flat stockinette-stitch front
- Straight pin
- Scissors
- Embroidery floss in 6 colors that contrast with the sweater
- Embroidery needle

1 Decide where you want the vertical stripes on the sweater; place a pin to mark where the stripe is nearest the sweater center. Cut 24-inch lengths of embroidery floss. Thread the needle with the color you want to be nearest the center of the sweater.

2 On the inside of the sweater, knot the floss end to the shoulder seam as close to the pin as possible. At the pin, push the needle to the front side of the sweater.

3 Using a duplicate-stitch, stitch the first vertical stripe. If you need to use additional floss, knot the ends neatly on the inside of the sweater. Do not pull the floss tightly, or the knots will pull through to the right side. Trim the tails.

4 Work each additional stripe in the same manner, skipping one row of the sweater stitches between each duplicate-stitch stripe.

5 To accent the collar, use two plies of floss and make one large stitch near the collar edge. Knot the ends together. Trim the floss ends leaving ½-inch tails to resemble small tassels. Work stitches around the entire collar, spacing stitches evenly apart and alternating floss colors.

57

Ribbon Embroidery Box

Keep treasured family heirlooms in this charming box. Or, create this special box to give on that sentimental matrimonial day to hold the garter, a flower and other mementos. A papier-mâché box and ribbon embroidery flowers on fabric combine beautifully to complete the project. You can line the inside of the box with fabric or just paint it.

TOOLS & MATERIALS

- Iron-on transfer pencil
- Tracing paper
- Iron
- Cotton fabric (5 by 7 inches)
- 1 yard crème embroidery floss
- Floss needle
- 1 yard each of the following ⅛-inch wide (4 mm) Bucilla/Plaid silk embroidery ribbon:
  - Light Coral, Dark Peach, Fern Green and Gold
- Silk embroidery ribbon needle
- No. 12 flat paintbrush
- Jade Green acrylic paint
- Cardstock (3¼- by 5¼-inch)
- Scissors
- Cream-colored papier-mâché box (5 inches long by 3 inches wide by 2½ inches high)
- Cotton quilt batting (5 by 7 inches)
- Hot glue gun and glue sticks
- White velvet piping (18 inches)

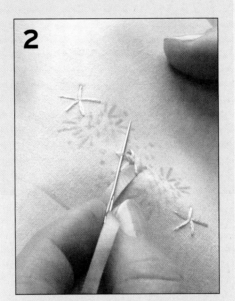

1 Using iron-on transfer pencil, trace pattern onto tracing paper. Iron pattern to center of fabric. Using embroidery floss, make five long stitches equally spaced in a ½-inch circle to create the spider's web rose stitch. Use Light Coral silk embroidery ribbon for the two outer roses. Starting in center, weave up and under spider's web stitches continuing to the outer edge to create each rose. Use Dark Peach for the center rose.

2 Using the lazy daisy stitch and Light Coral silk embroidery ribbon, create four rosebuds. Using the same stitch and Dark Peach silk embroidery ribbon, create four more rosebuds. Add two stitches of Fern Green silk embroidery ribbon to each side of rosebud base.

Using the French knot stitch and Gold silk embroidery ribbon, add knots around roses and rosebuds.

Using the loop stitch and Fern Green silk embroidery ribbon, add leaves to fill in void areas between roses and rosebuds.

Paint lid edge Jade Green. (If base is not pre-painted, you may paint the box base a color of your choice.)

3 Be sure cardstock is cut to size of the box lid. Cut batting to fit cardstock and secure with glue. Glue edges of fabric to underside of cardstock. Glue cardstock to top of box lid. Glue piping around edge of fabric and lid.

Appliqué Fall Sweatshirt

$$$

*S*elect various sizes and shapes of fall leaves to make a template for an appliqué that you stitch onto any fall sweatshirt. This project livens up even the plainest colored sweatshirt, and gives your garment a fun, seasonal theme.

TOOLS & MATERIALS

- Dried fall leaves or pattern
- Cardstock
- Pencil
- Scissors
- Heat-n-Bond fusible fabric (fusible on two sides)
- Iron
- Several scraps of fall-colored fabric
- Sweatshirt
- Craft fuse (fusible on one side)
- Pins
- Embroidery hoop
- Embroidery needle
- Embroidery floss in fall colors

1 Find several sizes or shapes of leaves and dry them in an air dry flower press or microwave flower press so that they are very flat. Place the leaves on cardstock; trace each one to make a template. Cut out the leaf template with scissors. Lay several leaf templates together and on top of each other to make arrangement. Use a piece of fabric behind the leaves to tie the shapes together. Use the cardstock leaf template and a pencil to trace the pattern onto the paper side of fusible fabric. Cut out the leaf shape leaving at least a ¼-inch edge of paper all around. With a hot, dry iron, press the pattern piece, fusible side down, onto the wrong side of a fall-colored scrap of fabric. Repeat for each leaf template using different-colored scraps of fabric. Cut out the fabric shapes and remove the paper from the back of the fusible fabric.

2 Arrange the square or round piece under the leaves on top of the front of a zipper-front sweatshirt or round-neck sweatshirt. Once you have the shape and design you want, remove them from the sweatshirt and place them on the fusible side of a piece of craft fusible fabric. Cut the craft fuse around the pattern grouping leaving an extra ½-inch all around the edges. Arrange the leaf grouping on the front of the sweatshirt making sure the fusible side is against the sweatshirt and the fabric side is displayed. Pin all pieces in place. Place the piece of craft fuse on the inside of the sweatshirt directly under the leaf grouping and pin in place. With a hot, dry iron, press the pattern pieces to the outside of the sweatshirt and the craft fuse to the inside of the sweatshirt.

3 Depending upon the thickness of the sweatshirt and pattern pieces, place a large embroidery hoop around the leaf grouping to hold the pattern firmly in place. Using an embroidery needle and two strands of complementary colored embroidery floss, stitch a blanket stitch around the outside of the leaves and the background fabric. Stitch the vein of the leaves in the center of each leaf pattern using the backstitch. Ensure all fabric on both sides is securely in place. If not, tack down with a slip stitch. Remove the hoop and press the sweatshirt with a hot iron to remove the wrinkles.

Hand-Stitched Lapel Pin

U se your favorite tiny stamp to create a simple, hand-stitched pattern that makes a great lapel pin.

TOOLS & MATERIALS

- Scissors
- Cutting mat
- Ruler
- Scrap of light-colored fabric
- Tiny square stamp
- Washable stamping ink
- Embroidery hoop
- Embroidery needle

- Embroidery floss
- Towel
- Iron
- Rotary cutter
- Light-colored cardstock
- E6000 glue or decoupage glue
- Lapel stick pin

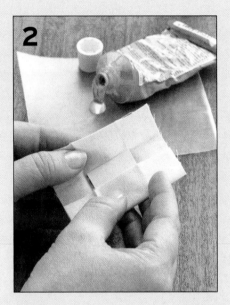

1 Cut a 4-inch square of linen or light-colored fabric. Using a tiny square stamp (no larger than 1 to 2 inches) and a washable stamping ink pad, stamp the pattern onto the center of the fabric square. Place the fabric in a small embroidery hoop keeping the fabric stretched tightly. Using a needle and 1, 2 or 3 strands of embroidery floss, stitch the pattern onto the fabric with the backstitch, satin stitch or French knot. Rinse the stitched fabric in warm water to remove the washable ink. Blot dry with a towel and press with a hot iron to remove the wrinkles and dry the fabric.

2 Cut cardstock in several small squares the same size as the stamp pattern using a rotary cutter, mat and ruler. Place the cardstock square in the center of the stitched picture with the wrong side of the stitching facing the cardstock square. Press the fabric over the cardstock, one side at a time, being sure to bend the fabric right at the edge of the stitching. Trim off excess fabric on all sides so that the cut edge just barely reaches the opposite side of the cardstock square. If cardstock is not very thick, use E6000 glue or decoupage glue to glue 2-3 cardstock squares together, one on top of the other. Place the cardstock square in the center of the pressed fabric and glue all four sides to the cardstock, one side at a time. Smooth the fabric so it is neat and straight. Allow to air dry for 2-3 hours.

3 Glue a lapel stick pin to the back of the hand-stitched square using E6000 glue. Allow to air dry overnight. Place the pin on the lapel of your jacket or blouse.

Handmade Greeting Card

*L*ayered papers and simple embroidery floss stitches combine to create lovely floral note cards you'll be proud to send.

TOOLS & MATERIALS

- Scissors
- Coordinating paper scraps: 3 colors for flower and 1 or 2 for leaves
- Flat plastic foam piece, such as Styrofoam
- Safety pin
- Sewing needle with large eye
- Embroidery floss in desired color
- Tape
- Contrasting paper ¼- to ½-inch smaller than card front
- Additional backing paper, if desired, ¼-inch smaller than above
- Glue stick
- Cardstock, folded in desired size of card

1 Using the photo as a guide, cut an oval from the desired paper for the inner petals of the flower. Cut five evenly spaced notches from the edge.

2 Hold the flower shape on top of the paper for the outer petals. Holding the layers together, cut around the oval, including the notches, leaving narrow borders.

3 Cut a flower center.

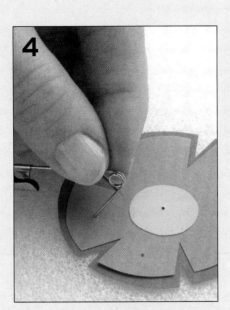

4 Layer the flower pieces; place on foam. Using a safety pin, poke a hole in the center through all layers. Poke a hole in the center of each petal.

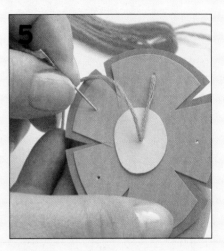

5 Thread needle with floss. From the back of flower pieces, bring needle through the center until the tail is ¼ inch long. Tape it to the back of the flower. Insert the needle through the hole in a petal. Continue stitching until all petals have one long stitch. Leave a short tail on the back; tape in place.

6 Cut leaves and stems, if desired. Poke two holes in each piece using the technique in Step 4. Stitch the leaves and stem to the top background paper, taping the floss ends on the back. Glue the flower in place.

7 Glue the decorated paper to a second backing paper, if desired, and mount on the cardstock. To trim envelope, cut a paper strip and glue onto envelope flap.

Paper Crafts and Scrapbooking

Paper crafts—which can mean almost any craft involving paper or even cardboard— include the categories of scrapbooking, card making, making paper, papier-mâché, and folding and cutting paper for design.

Scrapbooking

The fact that scrapbooking is one of the most popular and fastest growing crafts explains the volume of scrapbooking supplies filling craft store shelves. Scrapbooking keys into families who want to connect with their past and preserve memories for the future. To get started scrapbooking, you'll need (and want) some basic supplies including: an album or journal; white paper and colored cardstock (double-sided patterned paper is also available); die-cuts; frames and tags; borders; templates; punch art; stickers; page protectors; glue stick or other adhesive; decorative-edge scissors; punches; markers; and, of course, family pictures and mementos. To avoid the yellowing, browning and brittleness of aging, all items must be acid free.

You can make decorative papers, shapes and frames in a variety of ways. Numerous different punches, decorative-edge scissors and templates are available. Some templates involve a cutting and cropping system or an embossing system. Some embossing templates are used with a light box.

You can choose to purchase a start-up kit that supplies some of the basics. A kit offers an easy way to determine what tools and effects you like to use. After you become familiar with the processes and you "get hooked," you may find yourself buying many more tools and supplies. Beyond supplies, you'll find an unlimited variety of embellishments to buy or create.

Get started on scrapbooking with basic supplies.

To discover the types of embellishments that are available, just spend some time browsing at a craft store.

Embellishments include decorative tiles and tags, stamps, stickers, die-cuts, wire, dried flowers and trims (such as feathers, yarns, sequins, beads, buttons and ribbon). You may also use items from nature—leaves, bark, cedar boughs or raffia—or add fabric, stitching, embroidery, buttons, decorative painting, stamping, gilding and more. In addition to single embellishments, you will also find "theme packages" that include items focused on a theme, color or design.

With scrapbooking, planning is important and steps are sequential and easy. First, choose a subject (a family vacation, for example) and spread out photographs and suitable mementos. Organize items into interesting categories. Save each in a large labeled envelope. Work with one envelope group at a time, selecting the most interesting items or the best photo. Choose enough items to fill the page as desired. You will probably want to crop some of your photos to display them in a different size or shape for visual interest or to focus on the most important part of the image. To crop a photo, lay a cut-out shape or template on the photo, trying different angles. When you're satisfied, use the template to draw the shape onto the photo before cutting.

The next step is to decide which background paper to use for the base of your photo display. White always works well, colors bring out details, or the many themed papers add interest. Punches or decorative-edge scissors can help you create unique borders and trims. For dimensional effects, try chalking: Use a cotton swab to apply chalk around edges. Tearing paper edges of papers also creates interest. Don't forget to plan for titles or headings and any journaling. You can add text with templates, stickers, computer-generated text, cut-out letters or writing freehand. Determine how you will use any additional embellishments.

Be sure to lay out the entire page before affixing anything permanently.

A rotary paper trimmer or cutter is a good investment for card making.

When you're satisfied with a layout, first glue photos to their mats, then glue the background paper to the page. Finish gluing all elements to the page, overlapping as planned.

Digital scrapbooking is also becoming popular. The planning and the design process is similar, and you can do all or part of digital scrapbook projects with scrapbooking programs that are available for the computer. You can use an

existing basic digital template or create your own. Digital embellishments are also available.

Card Making

A natural extension of scrapbooking, card making utilizes many of the same tools, materials and techniques as scrapbooking. For cards as well as scrapbooks, you can also make use of additional crafts, including ribbon embroidery,

You'll find many of the essential supplies for these projects right in your own home.

cross stitch, beading, needlepoint and stenciling.

Making Paper

Handmade paper offers opportunities for you to create unique papers for scrapbooking, card making and other paper crafts.

To make paper, you can use recycled paper (but not newspaper), partly-processed fibers called cotton linter (available for purchase in craft stores) or plant fibers. Paper made from each of these products looks and feels different. (Cotton linter, for example, creates a white, smooth paper that's good for writing.)

Most items you'll use for making paper are things you have around the house, but you'll also need a mold and deckle to make paper sheets. You can purchase a mold and deckle, but it is easy to make your own. The mold (the bottom half) consists of a wood frame (this can be a picture frame or stretcher frame) with fine-gauge aluminum mesh stretched over the frame and taped in place with waterproof tape. The deckle is a wood frame of the same size for on top. Rather than a plain rectangular frame, you could use wood molds in other shapes, an embroidery hoop with netting fabric or a shaped template within your mold. Other methods by which to shape paper pulp include embossing and casting using bowls, relief shapes or cookie or candy molds.

More advanced decorative and creative techniques involve tearing or stitching the edges or using paint or dye. Added elements—such as fibers, yarn, thread, string, plastic strips, wire, sequins, dried flowers, herbs, spices with seeds, leaves, pine needles, feathers and tissue paper—make each paper unique.

To finish the papers, they are sometimes pressed. You can do this with a purchased press, or simply make one from bricks or clamps and fiber board. Making paper from plant fibers is more complex, requiring an alkaline solution, a longer preparation process, and more tools, including a chopping board, wooden mallet, netting and glass container.

You'll find more detailed information on paper making tools and procedures in the Handmade Paper Portfolio project on pages 72-73.

Cutting, Pasting, Rolling and Folding Paper

Paper crafts that may or may not use some of the above techniques include paper collages, decoupage with papers, and using or making papier-mâché. Most of these involve the use of a paste mixture and layering and/or shaping. With papier-mâché, you can make an ever-popular piñata or create shapes to resemble fruit.

Cutting and folding merge together in many of these crafts. From old cards or purchased or handmade paper, for example, you can make boxes of all sizes. The Japanese culture includes one classic paper folding technique—origami—that is passed down through generations.

Unique embellishments add excitement!

Cut designs from paper range from a child's folded snowflake and paper chains or flowers to silhouettes and detailed cut designs. Some paper-cutting-and-folding crafts become very intricate, such as ones from Italy, Mexico, Denmark, Germany and Switzerland. Traditionally, these cut designs embellished manuscripts, marriage certificates or valentine cards. Today, you'll find cut paper designs on lampshades, shelf edging, book covers, boxes, or featured in elegant frames.

Rolled paper strips, or quilled designs, can help embellish Christmas ornaments, handmade cards, scrapbooks and more. The Quilled Floral Place Card on pages 82-83 is just one specific project idea using this technique.

Your creative options with paper are virtually endless!

$ $

Scrapbookers always need ideas for embellishments—everything from the elegant to whimsical—to adorn their pages. These ideas are sure to please … and to spawn other creative ideas for you.

TOOLS & MATERIALS

- Scissors
- Assorted pastel-colored foam sheets
- Fine line permanent black marker
- Glue
- Paper, light and dark green (8½ by 11 inches)
- Mini silver or gold star stickers
- Mini cotton balls, if desired

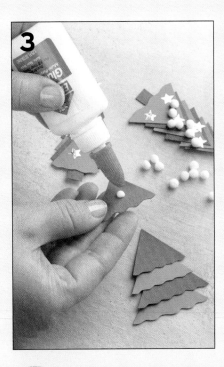

1 For a Valentines Page: Cut approximately fifty 1-inch hearts from assorted pastel-colored foam sheets. Using a fine line permanent black marker, write "conversation candy heart" phrases onto each heart such as Be Mine, Cutie, or Hot Stuff or write personal words and sentimental sayings about the person for whom the page is being created. Glue the hearts around the edge of a paper (8½ by 11 inches) to create a frame. Glue a photo to the center of the page.

2 For a Christmas Page: Cut a triangle out of light green paper that is approximately 1 inch wide at the base. Cut 5 more triangles each slightly bigger than the previous, alternating with a darker green colored paper every other triangle.

3 Cut scallop or wavy borders at the bottom edges of all the triangles. Glue the scalloped triangles together slightly overlapping each other. If desired, cut a trunk from the darker green paper. Embellish the tree with gold or silver stars for ornaments and one at the top for a tree topper. If desired, glue mini cotton balls onto the tree as garland. Use the tree to embellish a Christmas scrapbook page. If desired, make additional trees to create a Christmas winter wonderland.

*C*reate a beautiful expression of handcrafted art with a craft that crosses cultures and centuries. Use scraps of paper, potpourri, glitter, sheet music and paper images to designing a unique portfolio of handmade papers for a journal or sketchbook.

TOOLS & MATERIALS

- 1 cup of scrap papers (can include tissue paper, office paper, wrapping paper, sheet music, paper images or photos)
- Water
- Blender
- White glue
- ¼ cup potpourri
- Glitter
- Plastic tub larger than frame size
- Deckle
- Screen (wood frame covered with wire mesh)
- Old towel
- Sponge
- Hair dryer
- Iron and press cloth
- Strainer
- Plastic bag
- 2 sheets cardstock for front and back of portfolio cut ½ inch wider on top and sides than handmade paper size
- Hole punch
- Ribbon for portfolio closures

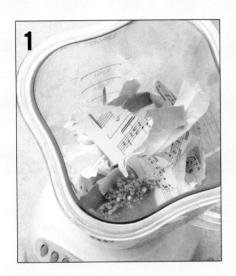

1 Tear paper scraps into 1-inch pieces. You will need one part scraps to four parts water. Fill blender ¾ full with warm water and paper scraps. Save small pieces that you may want to add as note pieces or images. Let paper soak for 15 minutes. Turn blender on blend for 15 seconds. Add a few drops of glue, potpourri and glitter and blend for another 10 seconds. Fill plastic tub half full with warm water. Add paper pulp from blender and extra torn scraps of small paper pieces. Stir mixture together.

2 Put the deckle on top of the wire mesh screen. Submerse the screen into the container of paper pulp. Draw back and forth in the water until the pulp is distributed evenly over the surface of the screen. Pull the screen straight out of the water and allow the water to drain away. Gently shake the screen and remove deckle from the screen.

3 Place towel on flat surface and flip the screen (paper side down) onto the towel. Gently sponge excess water from the back of the screen. Set hair dryer on low setting and lightly dry the paper. Lift screen off and peel away one corner of the paper from the screen, continue to peel away the paper until free from the screen. Transfer paper onto a flat dry surface to finish drying. An iron set on a low setting and a press cloth can be used to flatten paper completely. Collect excess pulp in a strainer and freeze in plastic bag to use again.

4 Center one sheet of handmade paper on cut cover of portfolio paper and glue in place. Place back sheet of portfolio cover under front portfolio cover. Use hole punch to punch two holes on one side of cover and one hole on opposite side punching through both front and back covers. Draw ribbon through holes. Insert loose handmade papers, and tie ribbon closures.

Make wonderful decorative baskets from greeting cards. Use new cards, or put ones you've received and saved to good use. Create beautiful memories and a functional basket.

TOOLS & MATERIALS

- Scissors
- 6 greeting cards, all approximately the same size
- Paper punch
- Yarn
- Poster board (11 by 14 inches)

1 Cut the top edge of the 6 greeting cards to form a curved edge.

2 Punch holes in two of the cards on all edges, approximately 1 inch apart. On the remaining 4 cards, punch holes approximately 1 inch apart on the two side edges as well as the bottom edge, leaving the top edge free of punches.

Using a long piece of yarn, lace 3 of the cards together (with the center card being the one punched on the top edge), making knots where necessary. Continue by lacing the next 3 cards together the same way.

3 Lace the 2 sections together. Form a rectangle shape with the laced cards. Place the rectangular shaped basket onto the 11 by 14-inch poster board and trace the bottom of the basket. Cut the traced rectangle out; this becomes the bottom of the basket. Make punches approximately 1 inch apart on the bottom piece. Line up the holes on the basket and tag board bottom and lace the two together.

Create a cute snowman out of paper clay. Paper clay is easy to shape and can air dry overnight. Add a little paint, decoupage and lacquer and you have an adorable adornment for your lapel.

TOOLS & MATERIALS

- Paper clay
- E6000 glue
- Paintbrush
- Craft paint (several colors as desired)
- Powdered rouge or blusher
- Decoupage
- Spray lacquer
- Lapel pin

1 Tear off a small piece of paper clay and roll it into a ball. Gently press on a flat surface so that one side is flat and the other side is gently rounded. Press it into a circular or egg shape that resembles a snowman head. Press the clay in irregular places to resemble a handmade snowball. Tear off another smaller piece of clay and shape a tiny clay hat and carrot nose. Use your fingernail to press tiny lines into the carrot shape to make it look more realistic. Let dry overnight. If possible, turn every few hours to ensure even drying. If the hat is made in two pieces, use a dab of E6000 glue to stick them together before painting.

2 Using a small paintbrush and craft paint, paint the hat and carrot. If preferred, also paint the "ball" white; let air dry. Using a dab of E6000, glue the "nose" position on the head, and the hat onto the snowman's head; let air dry. With a fine paintbrush and craft paint or a black fine point marker, paint or draw eyes and mouth on the snowman. Using your own powdered rouge or blusher, apply a small amount of blush to the cheek area of the snowman head.

3 Paint a layer or two of decoupage and let it air dry between coats. Spray with acrylic spray; let air dry. With E6000 glue, attach a lapel pin to the flat surface; let air dry.

*R*evamp an old watch face with paper beads created from your favorite scrapbooking paper. The possibilities are endless.

TOOLS & MATERIALS

- Paper trimmer
- Printed paper with coordinating prints (12 by 12 inches)
- Paper glue
- Bamboo skewer
- Paintbrush
- Paper glaze
- Measuring tape
- Pencil
- Stylus/paper awl
- Scissors
- Stretch elastic cording (0.5 mm)
- Crimp beads (silver No. 1)
- Crimping tool/needle-nose pliers
- Spacer beads (silver 5 mm)
- Watch face

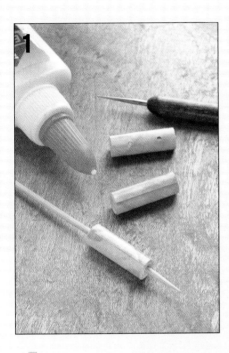

1 Using the paper trimmer cut paper into 1-inch strips. Starting ½ inch from one end, spread glue evenly onto the back of paper strip. Lay bamboo skewer perpendicular to the end of paper strip; roll paper tightly around skewer. Add additional glue to end of strip. Remove skewer and let bead dry. Repeat with additional strips. 12 to 14 beads are required for the project, depending on wrist size. Fill skewer with finished beads, leaving one end free to hold. Paint beads with a coat of paper glaze. Let dry. Repeat with additional layer of glaze. Let dry. Using measuring tape and pencil, place a mark on the side of bead ¼ inch from each end. Use stylus/paper awl to pierce 2 holes through each bead.

2 Cut a 16-inch piece of elastic cording. Add a crimp bead to cording. Wrap cording around end of watch face and back through crimp bead. Use crimping tool to close crimp bead.

3 Alternate adding paper beads and spacer beads to elastic cording ending with a paper bead. Add a crimp bead. Wrap cording around opposite end of watch face, thread cord back through crimp bead. Use crimping tool to close crimp bead. Thread cording back through all beads and around opposite end of watch face. Tie a double knot. Hide ends of cord by threading through two beads; add a drop of glue. Trim excess cord. Repeat instructions 6 through 8 to complete the second side of watchband.

Take a little time, but not a lot of money, to create handcrafted gift cards. They add a special touch to all gifts for all kinds of occasions.

TOOLS & MATERIALS

- Scissors
- Ruler
- 1 piece red-colored cardstock with a polka dot design on one side and a solid color on the other (12 by 12 inches)
- Deckle-edge scissors
- 1 piece black and white mini-diamond paper (8½ by 11 inches)
- White glue
- 1 piece "dictionary" paper (8½ by 11 inches)
- 5 inches of ½-inch-wide green ribbon
- E6000 glue
- 3 mini sunflowers with long wire stems
- Rounded toothpick
- 1 piece cream-colored cardstock (8½ by 11 inches)
- Decorative bow

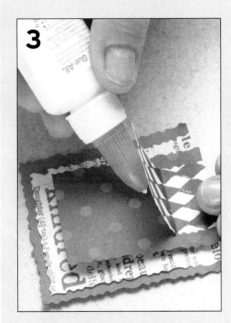

the ¾ inch part on the back of the card, and the longer part over the red card stock front flap.

1 Cut the red cardstock paper into a piece slightly larger than 5 by 2½ inches. Fold it in half with the polka dots on the outside. Using the deckle scissors, trim away 3 edges from one side. On the other side, cut away ⅜ inch from each of the three sides to create a smaller, front flap.

2 Using the deckle scissors, cut out one piece of black and white mini-diamond paper measuring 2½ by 1¼ inches. Fold over ¾ inch on one of the long ends. Apply a small amount of glue to the black and white mini-diamond paper on both sides of the fold. Place the fold point over the red cardstock fold, with

3 Using the deckle scissors, cut one piece of the "dictionary" paper to fit the inside of the card, with ⅛ inch of the red showing around the edges. Wrap the green ribbon around the front red cardstock and mini-diamond flap, about 1 inch from the top, and adhere it in the back of the front flap using a couple of drops of E6000 glue.

4 Pull the stems of 2 mini sunflowers through the top of the ribbon, and wrap the wire stems around a toothpick to create a spiral wire end. Spiral the wire onto the third mini sunflower, and hot glue it in the middle of the ribbon between the other flowers. Pull the wire ends out and curve them slightly.

5 With the deckle scissors, cut out a 2¼- by 1½-inch rectangle of cream-colored cardstock; fold it in half. Glue cardstock on inside of the card for a writing surface. Fashion a decorative bow for the top of the card and hot glue it in place.

U se the age-old technique of quilling to create simple and elegant flowers to adorn the front of place cards.

TOOLS & MATERIALS

- Paper shredder
- Heavy cardstock paper (8½ by 11 inches), assorted colors for flowers and leaves
- Scissors
- Corsage pin or thick quilting pin
- Glue
- Heavy cardstock paper (8½ by 5½ inches), white or light colored for place cards

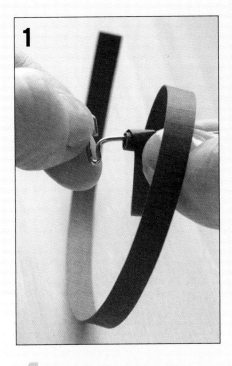

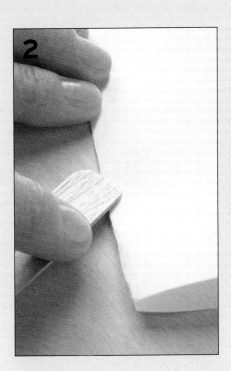

1 Shred strips of colored paper using a paper shredder that cuts strips ⅛ to ¼ inch wide. Cut strips into 5- by 8-inch lengths. Grasp the pin between your thumb and index finger. Moisten the end of the paper strip slightly or make a soft fold to help make rolling the paper strip around the pin easier. Start by rolling one end of the paper around the pin. Roll the first few times around the pin very tightly to ensure that the finished quill will be neat. Loosen the remaining rounds slightly, but keep the tension even for a neat, curving shape to the quill. Hold the shape securely and glue the end of the strip in position. Slip the quilled shape off the pin.

2 Make many different-colored quilled circles; these will be the basic shape to create the flowers for the place cards. Fold the 8½- by 5½-inch paper in half crosswise; this will become the place card.

3 To create the flowers for the front of the place cards, use one white quill for the flower's center and glue five colored quills around the outside edge of center piece. Use the quills in a round shape or make a looser circle and pinch both edges into an eye shape for a different look. Glue the flowers to the front of the place cards and write the name of the person on the front. Cut leaves from green cardstock, if desired.

Jewelry and Beading

Beading is very popular and ranges from very simple to very complex. Simple wire techniques used by themselves or incorporated with beads can create a great number of jewelry ideas.

Basic wire techniques can be used by themselves or incorporated with beads to create a variety of jewelry ideas. Wire shaping techniques require a minimal number of tools, but some practice. As is important in any craft, the right tools and materials are important.

Versatile beading techniques range from ultra-simple to creatively complex. Beading can involve stringing; needle weaving; weaving using a small loom; beading on surfaces; combining beads with wire; or adding beads to crocheted or knitted projects. You may purchase beads or try your hand at crafting them from oven-baked clay or paper. Follow your inspirations and create your own designs or follow project instructions in books or booklets you find.

Wire Jewelry

Wire used in jewelry making comes in silver, gold, brass and copper. Buy annealed wire, which is softened, making it easier to work with. Less expensive brass and copper wires are perfect for beginning jewelry makers. Sized by gauge, the wire most commonly used for jewelry ranges from 18 to 26 gauge; the higher the gauge, the finer the wire. For projects that incorporate beads, or for projects in which you will create small coils or bend wire intricately, use a finer gauge wire (26 and up).

Findings

Findings include such items as clasps, chains, ear wires and earring studs, pin backs, charms, jump rings, crimp beads and eyeglass loops.

Findings are components used to connect, hold and close jewelry pieces.

The different types of clasps are too numerous to discuss here thoroughly.

Choose a clasp that will accent or complement your wire or bead jewelry and that will also secure your jewelry items for wearing. Most clasps are available in base metals and may be plated, filled, brass, sterling silver, or copper. Clasps can be decorative or very simple. For bracelets or dangle earrings, consider decorative clasps as part of the piece's design.

Jump rings, crimp ends and crimp beads are integral to many jewelry pieces. A jump ring or crimp end connects the clasp to the bead strand. Crimp beads secure cording where a knot would not hold. End caps and headpins are other important jewelry making pieces. Most beaded necklaces begin and end with end caps. Headpins are commonly used to string one or more beads together for dangles, earrings, or to be attached to a chain.

Chain styles include ball-and-chain or linked chains. You will find chains in the same metals as most findings. Craft and beading stores also offer a wide variety of charms that you can add to many jewelry items.

Tools and Equipment

While you're stringing beads or organizing and designing with beads, a bead board works well to hold the beads in a line or in place. A bead mat, made from material similar to polar fleece, is a good surface to work on. You can purchase a bead mat or cut your own (about the size of a placemat) from polar fleece.

A bead board and pliers are a necessity for jewelry and beading projects.

You will need pliers, especially when you work with any wire component of jewelry making. You'll want at least two types of pliers; most commonly used are round-nose (or needle-nose) and flat-nose (or chain-nose). Round-nose pliers do not have grooves for gripping, so they will not leave a mark on the wire. Use a round-nose pliers for curving wire and looping ends of headpins. Use a flat-nose pliers for opening and closing jump rings and

for gripping, crimping and holding wire. Some pliers also feature a wire cutter. A spring motion will help make a pliers easier to control.

If your pliers do not include a wire cutter, you will need a separate wire cutting tool. Other necessities include a sharp pair of scissors, a ruler and good lighting. To remove sharp edges or bumps from wire jewelry, you'll need a small metal file; a 4-cut equaling nee-

dle file is a good size and shape for this purpose. Also helpful are an awl, tweezers, glass and bead adhesives, and clear nail polish.

Beads

Sized in millimeters, beads also vary in shape and texture. Bead materials include stone, metal, glass, ceramic, plastic, oven-baked clay and miscellaneous materials such as wood, seeds,

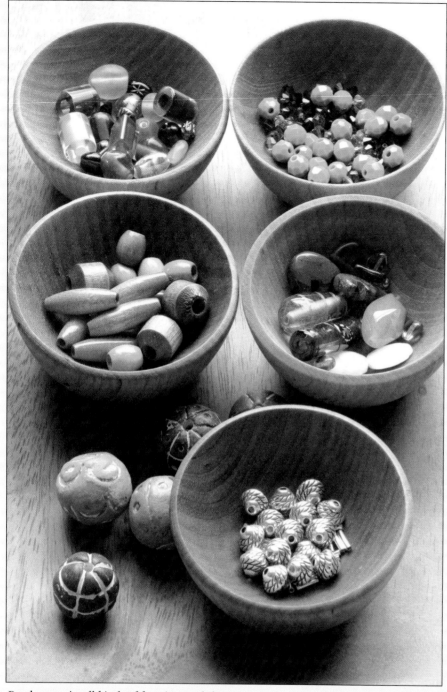
Beads come in all kinds of fun sizes and shapes.

and shape of beads needed; however, playing with the sizes, shapes and colors at the store is the best way to make decisions. At bead specialty stores many of the beads are loose. Craft stores typically sell beads in packages.

Use combinations that create a focal point of a larger or unique bead within the design. In most cases, it's desirable to vary bead sizes and shapes. For inspiration in color selection, look at fabric prints or nature for good color combinations.

Making Beads

The most common bead making material is oven-baked or polymer clay, such as Fimo or Sculpey. It is easy to shape and design, and you can bake it in a home oven. You can also make beads at home using paper techniques.

Thread and Needles

Thread selection must be appropriate to the project and the bead. Other thread considerations include its strength, color (if it will show, such as in a hand-tied necklace) and size (what will best fit the size of the bead hole). Wax is also used to make thread stronger, slide better and tangle less. When you go to purchase thread and needles, take a sample of the project's beads with you.

Traditional stringing materials include beading cord or beading string as well as silk or nylon thread. Elastic beading cord, memory wire, fine braided wire, leather, mastic (twisted cord), monofilament, fine gauge wire and elastic line are also popular stringing materials.

Beading thread sizes are labeled with letters, with A being heavier and D finer. When strength matters, select thread size based on bead weight. If you're using bugle glass or crystal beads, use the fine braided wire; these

shells, 'mother-of-pearl', amber and pearls.

Beads come in a variety of shapes, most commonly round, oval, disc, tube, convex, concave and square. Beads are also labeled with names for the positions they fill—rondells, crimp and spacers, for example. Within these groups you'll find commonly used beads, such as seed beads, bugle beads,

pony beads, drop beads, crystals and specialty beads like fetishes and shaped beads. The variety of beads available is endless.

Bead selection—size, material and color—is personal. The beads you choose and the sequence in which they are used makes each project special and unique. Spend time on these decisions. Most bead projects will indicate the size beads cut thread easily. If you're working on a fabric surface, regular sewing thread works best.

Longer than most needles, beading needles are very fine so that they fit through holes in small beads. Two common beading needle sizes are 10 and 12. Extra long needles are available, allowing you to "load" beads on the needle at once for projects like fringe. For some beads, embroidery needles in size 11 or larger work well.

A number 10 quilting needle may work well for finely drilled stones.

Knots

Some common knots used in beading are square knot, overhand knot and half hitch. (Illus. A, B and C). A dot of clear nail polish works well to seal a knot. You may also use clear nail polish to hold ends of twisted thread together. For holding monofilament or heavier thread, crimp beads work well.

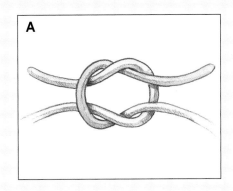

A

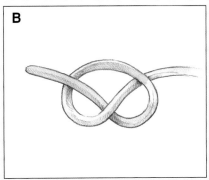

B

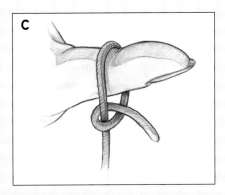

C

Helpful Tips

The easiest way to work with beads is to place them in a flat bowl or container or on your mat; use the needle tip to pick them up. Trying to hold each bead to put the needle through the bead hole is an unnecessarily slow process.

To help eliminate static electricity among glass beads, place a moistened paper towel, wrung out a bit, over the flat container of beads before use. If your glass beads are stored in a plastic bag, settle the beads down by blowing into the plastic bag lightly before you begin using them.

A variety of stringing materials is available for beading and jewelry making.

Memory Wire Bracelet

$

These bracelets are easy and fun to make at your special birthday party, scout meeting or sleepover. But remember: Kids of any age will enjoy making them … and wearing them.

TOOLS & MATERIALS

- Round-nose pliers
- Memory wire bracelet lengths
- 1 package silver Celestial charms
- 1 package each Glass Matte Striped and Autumn Glow Matte beads
- Flat-nose pliers

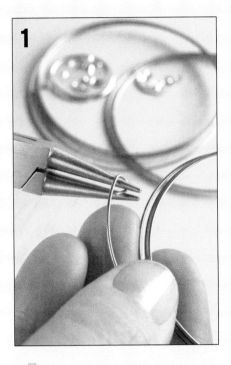

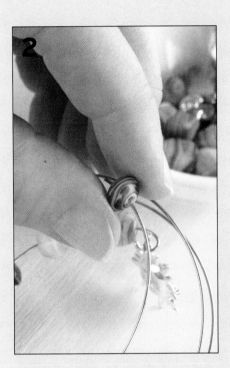

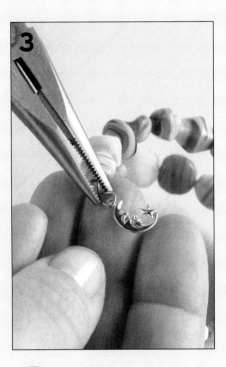

1 Using the round-nose pliers, make a loop at one end of the memory wire and slip on a charm. Close the loop tightly.

2 String on enough beads to fill the wire leaving ½ inch at the end.

3 With the flat-nose pliers, make a loop at the end, slip on a charm and close the loop tightly.

4 For variation, if you want the bracelet charms along the length of the bracelet, make a loop at one end and string on beads, adding 4 charms along the length to within ½ inch of the end. Make a loop at the end; close tightly.

Clay Bead Bracelet

*T*oday's oven-baked polymer clays make it possible for you to custom-design beads and jewelry to match any outfit. You'll have fun, but this project is also easy enough for kids!

TOOLS & MATERIALS

- Polymer clay in black, white, salmon and red
- Straight-edged razor
- Paper clip

- Aluminum foil
- Pie pan
- Stretchy bracelet cord

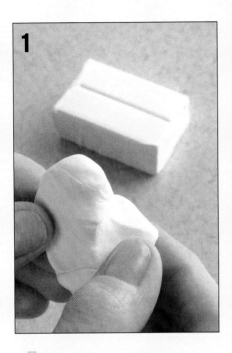

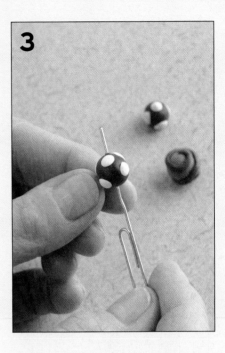

1 Cut off ¼ of black clay and condition it. (Polymer clay must be conditioned before it is used. Cut off a piece of clay, warm it in your hand, and work it together between your fingers until it is pliable. Begin with very clean hands. Some lighter colored clays, like white and yellow, pick up dirt and lint from your hands.) Roll clay into a long "snake," approximately ¼ inch wide. Cut into the same-sized pieces, approximately ¼ inch wide. Condition a smaller piece of white clay and roll it into a long snake, approximately ¹⁄₁₆ inch wide. Cut into the same sized pieces, approximately ¹⁄₁₆ inch wide.

2 Roll a black piece of cut clay into a ball. Roll 6 white pieces into miniature balls and press them around the black ball. Roll again in your hand to smooth the black and white polka-dotted ball. Carefully press paper clip through center of the ball to make a bead. Make sure bead is completely round before placing it into an aluminum foil-lined pie pan. Make 10 black and white polka-dotted beads.

3 Condition salmon and red clays in the same way as described above. Roll salmon-colored clay into a long "snake," approximately ¼ inch wide. Cut into the same-sized pieces, approximately ¼ inch wide. Condition a smaller piece of red clay, then roll it into a long, very thin "snake." Cut approximately 1½-inch pieces from the red snake. Press the red "snake" into a curly design on the salmon ball. Roll again in your hand to smooth the ball. Carefully press paper clip through center of the ball to make a bead. Make sure bead is completely round before placing it into pan. Make 10 salmon/red beads.

4 Follow the manufacturer's instructions to bake the clay. Remove pan from oven, then cool beads completely.

5 Wrap stretchy bracelet cord around your wrist and determine how you want the bracelet to hang. Add an extra inch and cut the cord. String beads onto cord and make a double knot. Cut off excess cord.

91

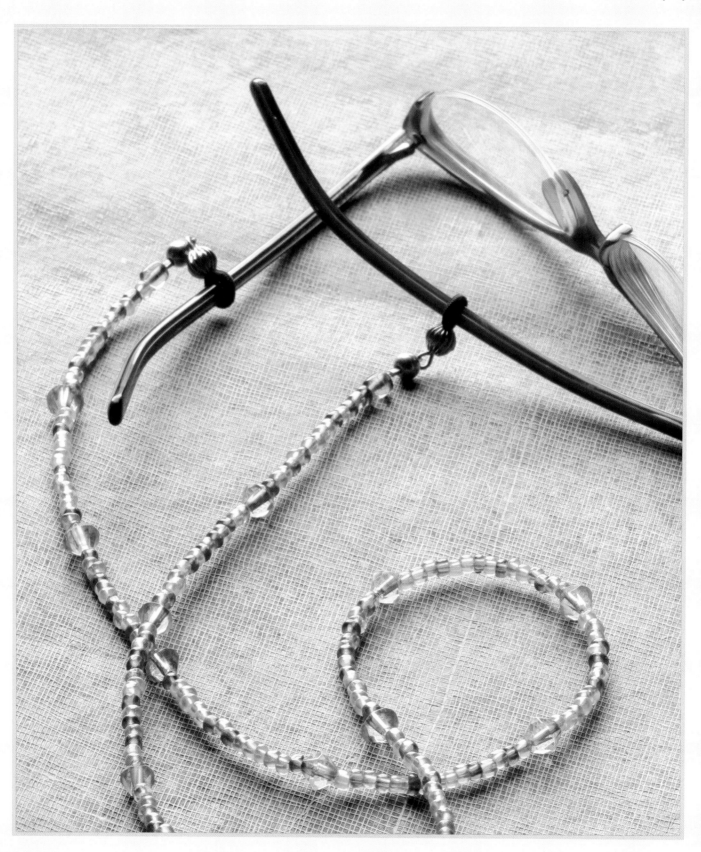

Keep your glasses in plain sight. Save time looking for those reading glasses. Be the envy of your friends, with this stylish beaded eyeglass keeper. Here's a stylish and creative way to keep track of those reading glasses you're always looking for. This project also makes a great gift idea.

TOOLS & MATERIALS

- Jewelry making tool kit with needle-nose pliers and wire cutter (may need common pin to unclog small beads)
- Tiger tail wire
- Seed beads and/or spacers in sizes, colors and styles of your choosing
- Scotch tape
- Crimp tube (either silver or gold)
- Eyeglass holder ends
- Super glue

1 With the wire cutter, cut a 30-inch piece of tiger tail wire. Some wire will be trimmed away in the final steps. Pre-arrange the beads and/or spacers in a design of your choosing. Tape one end of the wire so the beads do not fall off as you string them on the other end of the wire. Thread the beads on to the wire using the wire as if it were a needle. Once you have completed the length of beads, view the pattern to make sure it is what you want. To make changes, remove the beads and re-string the section you want to change. The finished eyeglass keeper is approximately 26 inches long. Make it longer or shorter, according to your personal preference.

2 Once you have strung the beads, remove the tape and thread a crimp tube on one end of the wire making sure the crimp tube is close to the last bead. Next, pass the wire through the metal loop of the eyeglass end. Turn the wire back into the same crimp tube and through as many of the beads in the string as you can. The extra wire helps strengthen the connection. Cinch up the wire through the beads and firmly crimp (flatten) the crimp tube with the needle-nose pliers. (As an option, place a dab of super glue on the wire around the crimp tube.) Be careful not to use too much glue as glue stiffens the craft work. Trim off the extra wire that you pulled through the beads with the wire cutter. Sparingly, place a dab of super glue inside the bead where the two strands of wire ended.

3 The second end is more difficult to do. Follow step 2 again. Thread the excess wire back through the crimp tube and beads at least 1 inch or more and let the wire exit between two beads. To keep the beads tight together, grasp the wire strand as it comes out of the strand of beads at the eyeglass metal loop and hold it tightly with your thumb and index finger. Pull the end of the excess wire with the needle-nose pliers, as you firmly hold the eyeglass loop. Cinch up the wire through the beads, crimp the tube and eyeglass end so that minimum wire is showing. Tightly flatten the last crimp tube with the needle-nose pliers. Place dabs of super glue as in step 2. Slide the eyeglass ends onto each sidepiece on your favorite pair of glasses.

Crystal Needlewoven Bracelet

*L*earn one new beading technique—the right-angle weave—and go from there to create this sparkling bracelet. Fireline thread is necessary because crystals easily cut any other beading thread.

TOOLS & MATERIALS

- Beading mat
- Fireline braided wire thread
- Size 12 beading needle
- 2-strand clasp
- Size 11 seed beads to match crystals (approximately 20)
- Crystals – approximately 97 (4 mm) or approximately 60 (6 mm)
- Scissors

1 Double thread needle with about 3 yards of braided wire thread. If the clasp has an insert that is depressed to insert—use that piece of clasp in step 3. Pick up 3 seed beads, one hole in clasp from the back side, 3 more seed beads, the second hole in the clasp through the front side, and one crystal. Pull all to approximately 3 inches from end of thread, leaving a 3-inch tail to be tied later.

2 Pick up 3 crystals and go through the crystal from step 1 again in the same direction. Pull them taut to the original crystal forming a circle of 4 crystals. Continuing in the same direction, thread through the next 2 crystals, ending at "top" one or the one opposite the original crystal. Pick up 3 more crystals and continue by repeating until the bracelet is ½ inch shorter than desired length. If the bracelet is for you, put it on your wrist to determine the length (7 inches is a typical bracelet length).

3 Pick up 1 crystal, 3 seed beads, one hole in clasp from front side, 3 more seed beads, the other hole in the clasp from the back side. Go through crystal again and tie 2 or 3 half-hitch knots by putting the needle under the thread between crystals and looping the needle thread under needle and over tip of needle. Pull thread tight. Run thread through a few more crystals and tie a few more half-hitch knots. Cut thread. At the other end (the beginning) run the thread through several crystals and tie a few half-hitch knots. Cut excess thread.

Hand-Tied Beaded Necklace

$

96

*H*and tying is the traditional way to string necklaces of finer beads or pearls. It makes the necklace stronger and more fluid, and also prevents losing all the beads if the necklace does happen to break.

TOOLS & MATERIALS

- Beading mat
- Mastic thread
- 2 small beads with large hole
- 2 or more specialty beads (larger than stone beads)
- 72 (10-mm) stone beads
- Large needle
- Fingernail polish
- Scissors

1 Measure an amount of thread about 3 to 4 times the finished length of necklace. Thread one small bead approximately 3 inches from the end, then tie in a square knot. Add the desired specialty bead or beads, tying between with a square knot. From the other end, thread your stone beads. You can do all or a few at a time.

2 Tie a single overhand knot between each bead in the following way: Be sure bead is next to last bead. Create a circle with thread near bead, then bring the beaded end through circle. Do not pull knot tight before step 3.

3 Put a needle into the knot before pulling knot tight. Push needle toward the bead until knot and needle are tight to bead. Remove needle and push knot tight with fingernail. Bring next bead next to knot and repeat until the desired length. Finish the end with a specialty bead and small bead. Thread ends back through beads. Dab fingernail polish at last knot and cut excess thread. Do the same on the beginning end of necklace.

$

Combine twisted wire and beads to easily create these attractive earrings. With a few basic techniques and tools, and just a little practice, the possibilities are endless.

TOOLS & MATERIALS

- Wire cutter
- 26-gauge copper wire
- Masking tape
- Size 6 knitting needle (to be used as a mandrel)
- Needle-nose pliers
- Assorted beads
- Flat-nose pliers
- 2 ear wires

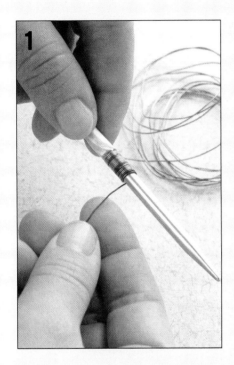

1 With wire cutter, cut approximately 60 inches of copper wire. Bend tip at a 45-degree angle and tape to knitting needle. Wrap wire tightly by twisting the knitting needle and guiding the wire onto the knitting needle. Coil very close together, holding wrapped wire taut as you go. Finished length of coils should be approximately 1¾ inches. You can do both wraps on the same needle, leaving the first in place. Remove coils.

2 Turn tips of wire into the coil. Cut a 4-inch length of wire and thread it through coil, pulling wire coil almost into a circle. Twist wires one full turn, by hand. To make wire for bead, cut a 3-inch piece of wire. With needle-nose pliers, twist the end of wire around nose point. Thread bead on wire. Repeat for other earring. Attach wire with bead to twist at top of coil, twisting 3 wires together, using flat-nose pliers. Cut excess wire from center wire. Attach to ear wire, by making a loop at top of center wire and putting it around ear wire and closing it. Twist the 2 extra wires into decorative circles.

3 A decorative way to make a dangle beaded earring is to create a flat coil at the end of the wire to hold the bead or beads. Try different combinations of beads. Try a short coil similar to the one in step 1, but just wrap it around the needle-nose pliers. Intersperse beads in the coil, if desired. Add as many beads in as many shapes, as desired, to wire created for earring. Attach to ear wire as in step 2.

Beaded Fringe Scarf

*M*ake your own exquisite beaded fringe to add to a hand-knit scarf, a purchased scarf, or to other fabric scarves or shawls. It's a touch of fun and style you'll love creating … and wearing. This is a great way to "personalize" a gift too.

TOOLS & MATERIALS

- Scarf
- Large safety pin
- Beading needles (size 10, 12 or longer)
- Nymo beading thread (match color of the scarf)
- Beading mat
- Blue and white seed beads (size 11)
- Larger beads (about 6 to 7mm)
- Seed beads (size 6 or 8)
- Iridescent or multifaceted beads (size 6 to 8)
- Scissors

1 Start with corner or end knit stitch of scarf. Place a safety pin in corner or end knit stitch. Thread needle with approximately 3 yards of doubled thread. Tie an overhand knot approximately 3 inches from the end. Go through the knit stitch with the needle, then between the tied ends of thread; pull tight.

2 Place enough beads on beading mat for several dangles, each in individual piles. Pick up 10 (size 11) blue seed beads on the needle and 1 larger seed bead. Push beads to base. Pick up 10 (size 11) white seed beads and 1 larger seed bead. Repeat. Be sure to count beads carefully. Put as many beads on the needle as comfortable. Before the last large seed bead is on the needle, add an iridescent bead and then the last large seed bead. Push beads tight and pick up largest bead, large seed bead and 3 seed beads. Push beads tight and hold dangle taut, putting needle back through last large seed bead, continuing through bead holes as far as possible. Continue back through beads to base or knit stitch.

3 Make a half-hitch knot at base and thread needle through to next knit stitch. Make another half-hitch knot. Do not pull thread tighter than the natural distance between knit stitches. For a loosely woven scarf, be very careful not to pull the thread too tight. Continue making dangles until there is only enough thread left to go through one more dangle. When that dangle is done, tie an overhand knot close to the base of the dangle and thread needle back through 10 to 12 beads; cut thread. Start next dangle as in step 1 and continue until all dangles are complete. Thread the beginning tails through needle and thread back through first dangle and cut thread. Finish all thread tails.

$ $

*D*ress up your bare feet for those lazy summer days at the beach, next to the pool or just in the yard. This sea glass and silver sea creatures ankle bracelet will look marvelous.

TOOLS & MATERIALS

- Ruler
- Silver chain
- Wire cutter
- Silver jump rings
- Silver sea charms – shell, starfish and
- sand dollar
- Silver head pins
- Silver metal oval beads (4- by 6-mm)
- Triangular turquoise glass beads
- Round-nose pliers

1 Measure 9 inches along the chain and cut so clasp is included. Remove jump ring and tag and place them on the other end of the 9-inch length (your chain might have a jump ring). Note: When opening a jump ring twist the ends. Do not pull apart.

2 Add jump rings to the three charms. Divide the chain in half and place one charm in the middle of the bracelet. Add other charms equally spaced between charm and clasp and charm and tag end.

3 On a head pin, place a silver oval bead and a turquoise bead. Bend pin at a right angle approximately ¼ inch above the beads. Cut pin leaving 1½ inches of the pin.

4 Using the round-nose pliers, curl the pin up to make a loop. Make 10 beaded elements.

5 Place 2 beaded elements evenly spaced between charm and clasp and between charm and tag end. Place three beaded elements between the center charm and the next charm. Make sure the loops are closed tightly.

Floral Arranging

Floral decorations come in many forms, all artistic and greatly varied. Floral design principles are similar, no matter the source of your elements—fresh, artificial or dried.

Fresh Flowers and Greens

Although today's silk flowers offer realistic alternatives to fresh blooms, nothing can replicate the fragrance of a fresh arrangement. You can arrange fresh flowers in arrangements of any size and can combine them with silk or dried elements. You'll find that floral shops carry a broad selection of fresh flowers year-round, but in-season blossoms or those from your own garden offer the easiest and most economical florals for arrangements.

No matter where your fresh flowers come from, cutting most stems on a diagonal will help them absorb water. For best results, cut roses under water. To help prolong the life of your fresh arrangement, keep the water fresh, changing it every few days. It also helps to use Aquafoam and floral preservatives (available at florist shops) and to keep arrangements in a cool location.

Compared with arranging silk and other artificial flowers, there are two main differences in arranging fresh flowers. First, the container you use must be able to hold water. Secondly, if you choose to use floral foam to steady the stems, you must select foam specifically for use with water (Aquafoam is one example). Without floral foam, it's a good idea to steady stems with a grid of tape across the top of a vase.

Fresh flowers bring beauty and life into any room.

Silk and Other Artificial Stems and Greens

"Silks" is a general term for any artificial materials used for floral decorating, including blossoms, bushes, berries, fruits and greens. But "silks" are not always made of silk. They usually have a wired stem making them flexible, sturdy and easy to work with. Silks with plastic stems or those available in bushes typically cost less.

Dried Naturals

Dried naturals—dehydrated from flowers, buds, leaves and fruits that were once living—offer a more textured, delicate look and more muted colors than silks. Dried naturals that you purchase may have been air dried, dried with a silica gel, or freeze dried. Dried stems, greens, grasses, seeds and pods are available in craft stores and specialty floral stores. Or you can dry your own florals at home using a drying product (such as silica gel) purchased from a craft store.

Dried naturals.

Tools

To arrange flowers, you will need a few basic tools including a heavy-duty wire cutter for cutting floral wire, stems and grapevine; a serrated knife for cutting floral foam; a sharp knife for cutting fresh flowers; and sharp scissors for cutting ribbons and other elements. Utility snips, an awl and a tape measure also come in handy.

Floral arranging tools.

Artificial flowers are quick, easy and beautiful.

105

Materials

Adhesives used in floral arranging include a glue gun with glue sticks; floral and stem tape; and, occasionally, craft glue. Waterproof florist tape allows you to attach floral foam to the container. Using hot glue that does not harden quickly allows you to move elements while arranging, before the glue dries.

To extend stem lengths, you can use floral wood picks or 16- to 20-gauge stem wire in a variety of lengths. Stem wire is also used to help hold elements in an arrangement. Florist's wire, another wire useful for holding things in place, comes wrapped around a "paddle." Floral pins help anchor moss and other elements in an arrangement.

For dried arrangements, floral foam traditionally comes in grayish brown blocks. For artificial and dried arrangements, green or brown floral foam is available in blocks, sheets or shapes. For silk arranging, floral Styrofoam—which can be glued easily—is available in sheets or in forms like cones, wreaths and balls. As mentioned above, you'll use a product like Aquafoam for fresh floral arrangements.

Foam holds flowers in place; mosses add texture and depth.

Mosses add texture and depth to arrangements. You will find a wide variety of mosses available: sheet moss (also called spagnum); green or decorator moss; reindeer moss; Spanish moss; and excelsior moss. Excelsior comes in green, brown and a golden tone. Choose a moss based on the look and texture you want.

To finish your arrangement, you may use a spray adhesive or glitter for a festive touch. An aerosol floral sealer applied to dried items helps preserve them. Other common finishes include aerosol paint for items such as pinecones and branches, as well as acrylic paint and wax-based paint for adding visual interest to leaves and petals.

Decorative notions include ribbon,

lace, raffia, cellophane, tissue, tulle, berries, birds and miniature fruits. Wired ribbon works well for draping or creating bows. Picks, which are individual blossoms or small floral groupings already on a wire, make it easy to add extra flowers to your arrangements. For more formal arrangements, you might use a garland or string of beads. Browse through craft or floral specialty stores for other ideas and items to enhance your arrangements.

Method

The most common and simple method for drying or preserving flowers is the "hang-dry" method. This involves hanging the flowers in small bunches in a well-ventilated, cool place for several weeks. Cut the flowers with a garden scissors or

clipper. Place flowers into a small bunch and secure with a rubber band. Hang the flowers from a nail or peg, being sure that air can circulate all around the bunch. To dry larger quantities of flowers, nail a 1- by 3-inch board, which is 30 inches in length, to an empty wall in a garage. Drill several ¼-inch-round holes into the board, about 6 to 8 inches apart. Purchase ¼-inch wooden dowels and place them into the holes. Place several bunches of flowers on one dowel. If the flowers are heavy, a larger hole and dowel can be used. The dowel will droop slightly, but this doesn't harm the drying process. Allow the flowers to hang for 2 to 3 weeks before using in an arrangement.

Include different sizes and shapes of flowers to add interest to an arrangement. Select flowers that are just about to bloom or have only partially bloomed.

Plan to dry a new crop of flowers every year and use them to replace arrangements annually.

Containers

Select containers as carefully as you do the floral elements of your arrangements. With the final arrangement in mind, consider the container's color, texture and size and whether you want a vessel that's traditional, country, contemporary or whimsical in style. The container you choose may expand beyond the traditional glass, pottery, ceramic or metal vase. Try arranging flowers in a basket, bowl, teapot, serving bowl, mason jar or old watering can. (If you use a porous container like an antique colander, for example, line it with heavy plastic or place a smaller plastic bowl inside.) Choosing a unique container can be a fun and creative part of the design.

Basic Design

Think about factors such as the room's decor, the season of the year, or the holiday or event you're commemorating. Your arrangement may have a basic seasonal theme or may be themed around an occasion. Focusing on a theme will help you determine the style of floral and accent elements to use.

Consider where you will place your arrangement. Will it serve as a centerpiece that will be seen from all sides? Will your arrangement adorn a sideboard or buffet, for example, that will be viewed from only three sides? Will you create a wall arrangement, such as a wreath or swag?

Once you have determined your arrangement's placement, consider the shape or form you want to create. For a centerpiece, a mound shape is typi-

Floral arranging containers come in infinite shapes and sizes.

cal; a linear arrangement shows some motion. Pay attention to the arrangement's size and shape in proportion to its position in the room. (Take care not to make a centerpiece too tall, for example, or an end table arrangement too large.)

Along with placement and form, consider the texture and color of your arrangement. Create varied texture by selecting various blossoms and other elements. Color is a personal preference but may often be dictated by the decor or occasion. You may prefer to stay with a single color group, or choose pleasing color combinations and group pieces while you shop.

Choose a large blossom or blossoms for a focal point and select medium-

sized secondary materials. Filler materials may include small flowers, line elements (such as foliage, twigs or wispy blossoms) and possibly special elements (a glass ball or feathers, for example). Visually balance your secondary and filler materials in weight, size, texture and color. While balance is important to an arrangement's design, your arrangement doesn't need to be symmetrical.

The process of creating an arrangement varies even among floral designers. Some insert the large focal flower first, and some insert the greens or line elements first. Follow individual instructions for an arrangement or follow project instructions for specific arrangements; or experiment to discover what works for you.

Dried Floral Wreath

*I*f you have your own flower garden at home or a fresh flower market close by, you have a ready supply of fresh cut flowers that you can dry and use on projects like this.

TOOLS & MATERIALS

- Wire cutter
- Wire
- Grapevine wreath
- Garden clipper
- Dried flowers
- Spray lacquer or floral preservative spray

1 Cut a 6- to 8-inch length of wire and twist it onto the back of the wreath. Hang the empty wreath on a nail in your garage at a level that you can easily see and reach from all sides. Break or cut a length of stem off of each flower, allowing a 5- to 7-inch stem. Remove the large leaf material and preserve the bloom on each stem you will use. Select several complementary colors and shapes of flowers.

2 Insert the more diffuse flowers like sea lavender or cloud larkspur in a half circle shape around the wreath on the right or left, according to your preference. Don't use glue to stick flowers to the wreath. It will be easier to remove the flowers later when you want to redo the arrangement. If you plan to decorate the entire wreath, place the diffuse flowers all around the circle of the wreath. Allow flower stems to just touch each other to give an open and airy look. Add statice, delphinium or globe amaranth to fill in the areas left open by the more diffuse flowers and add different colors to the arrangement.

3 Save the more unusual flowers for last. Globe thistle and sea holly have a very distinctive round, spiky shape and a silvery blue color that adds a finishing touch to any arrangement. Add these flowers in strategic places until you have the look you desire. Spray the entire arrangement with a spray lacquer or flower preservative spray. This prevents some of the breakage of flowers, preserves the flower color longer, and prevents the flowers from attracting dust.

Fresh Winter Arrangement

$ $

*T*his project makes a thoughtful holiday gift. There's nothing better than the vibrant color and robust aroma of fresh-cut materials to brighten up any home in winter.

TOOLS & MATERIALS

- Scissors
- Aquafoam – ⅓ brick
- Bowl of water
- 5 fresh cedar and pine stems
- Glass container or coffee mug
  (5 inches high)
- Waterproof floral tape
- 1 stem of fresh caspia, baby's breath or holly
- 3 fresh carnations
- Decorative glittery or garland wire (optional)

1 Cut foam to approximate size and soak in a bowl of water approximately 20 minutes or until saturated. Foam will darken. Meanwhile, prepare the greens. Break cedar and pine into 6- to 8-inch pieces. Remove lower needles and cut ends at sharp angle with scissors. Cut foam to fit the container. It does not need to fit snugly or be in a circle, just cut the corners off. Let it extend approximately 1 inch beyond the container. If foam is not high enough, place an additional piece of cut foam in the bottom of the container. Angle edges of foam to container edge. Tape with waterproof tape. Add water.

2 Insert greenery stems into foam, mostly around the outside. Allow some of them to hang over the edges of the container. Reserve some of the stems for later, including the smaller pieces.

3 Cut the carnation stems 6 to 8 inches. Hold them alongside the container, to determine the correct height and cut. Vary the height for interest, if desired. Insert the carnations into center area. Break off pieces of caspia and cut stem ends at an angle. Insert caspia, using varying sizes. Fill in, as needed, with additional small greens. Add twisted wire or garland, if desired.

Artificial Fall Arrangement

$ $

*T*his rustic fall arrangement will remind everyone of the falling leaves and all that nature has to offer. Just the raw ingredients are a delight to behold.

TOOLS & MATERIALS

- Serrated knife
- Floral foam for silk and dry floral arrangements – 1 brick
- Container (4 inches high by 5 inches in diameter)
- Glue gun and glues sticks (optional)
- Scissors
- Large fall hydrangea blossom stem
- Large pinecone with wire

- 16- or 18-gauge stem wire and floral tape
- Waterproof floral tape
- 5 or 6 leaves (seeded eucalyptus)
- 3 or 4 small blossom stems (wild daisy)
- 2-inch glass ball on wire
- Twigs
- Feathers (pheasant)
- Spanish moss
- Floral pins (optional)

1 With knife, cut foam to fit inside of the container. Angle it and cut corners if necessary. Two pieces may be needed. It should come to just below the top of the container. The foam may be glued in to make it more permanent, but glue is not necessary.

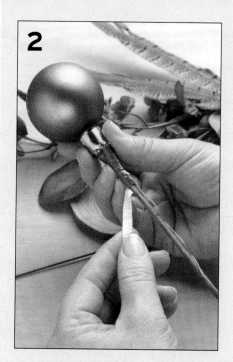

2 Cut large blossom stem to approximately 10 inches. Remove lower leaves. Place it in the center of the foam and push to the bottom. Add pinecone on stem next to blossom. If any stems or other elements need to be extended or strengthened, line up a wire stem with the complete length of stem and wrap with floral tape the length of the stem.

3 Add leaves around edges of arrangement. Add smaller flowers to fill in. When arrangement is filled in, as desired, add glass ball to balance pinecone. Add twigs and feathers in a few areas. Fill in the base of the arrangement with moss, poking it in around stems using a blunt object. Hold it in place if necessary with floral pins.

Spring Bouquet

*T*his artificial spring bouquet looks as good as a freshly picked one, but lasts much longer. It's perfect for spring, but suitable for any season at all.

TOOLS & MATERIALS

- 2 tall artificial greens – eucalyptus
- Tall artificial stems – delphinium, apple blossom
- Larger artificial blossom stem – lilac
- Medium artificial stems – chrysanthemum, carnation
- 4 wispy artificial stems – wild daisy, fuchsia

- Glass vase (11 inches high)
- Wire cutter
- Small teacup and saucer
- Florist wire
- Stem wire 18 inches (16- or 18-gauge)
- Glass and bead glue
- Marbles

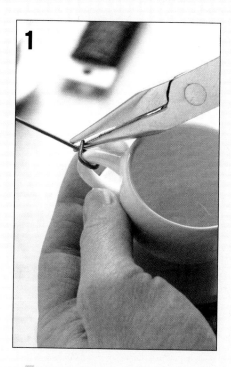

1 Place all stems in vase. Determine approximately how high you want the arrangement; trim stems. Prepare teacup by wrapping the end of stem wire around the handle and twisting. Glue teacup and saucer together; allow to dry according to manufacturer's directions. Place marbles in bottom of vase.

2 Working on a flat surface, group the tall stems and greens together in your hand. Add the large blossom stem. If desired, wrap stems with florist wire to hold in place. Next, add the medium stems. Continue adding stems, placing them to balance the color and weight of the arrangement.

3 Add stems that will hang down around edges of arrangement. Wire the arrangement together. Trim any stem ends that are too long. Place arrangement in vase; tweak as desired. Wire teacup to stem close enough to where bouquet is wired together.

Flower Time

*W*hen the sun shines, it's flower time with this creative craft! Combine the age-old art materials of clay and water, then sculpt the by-product into a flower holder hidden behind a decorative and useful sundial.

TOOLS & MATERIALS

- 1 sheet of Plexiglas
- Red self-hardening clay (32 oz.)
- Rolling pin or wooden dowel
- Dull knife
- Plastic bowl

- Water
- Toothpicks
- 1½-inch nail
- Acrylic paint
- Spray matte finish

1 Place one sheet of Plexiglas on hard level surface. Divide clay into two pieces, ⅓ and ⅔ pieces. Knead the larger piece of clay to distribute moisture and to make the clay more malleable. Roll clay into ball shape, then square off four sides by pounding each side onto the hard Plexiglas surface. Use a rolling pin or wooden dowel to flatten clay to a thickness of ¼ inch. Using a dull knife, cut two straight sides. For the curved top and bottom of the sundial, use a plastic bowl to outline the curve shape before cutting. Lightly moisten cut edges with water to smooth cutting lines.

2 Starting at the bottom of the sundial, use a toothpick to draw in time measures (VI, VII, VIII, etc.) and continue clockwise. Add radiating lines upward to the area where the sun will be placed. Take a small clay ball and flatten out with the palm of your hand. Use a toothpick to draw a sun face. Add extra clay for cheeks and nose to add dimension to the face. Use the nail to make a round hole for the mouth. Wet the back of this sun face to join it to the sundial surface. Add extra sunrays to join the radiating lines of the numbers with the rays of the sun. Flatten out another ball of clay to use for making leaves and grape motif. Again, use a small amount of water to join these to the sundial surface.

3 Roll out remaining ⅓ of clay onto Plexiglas to a thickness of ¼ inch. Cut a triangle shape out of the clay to be used for the back flower holder. Moisten two edges of the triangle and position on center, two inches from the top of the sundial. Press clay gently together joining holder to sundial. Use a nail to punch a hole for hanging on the top of the holder. Allow sundial to air dry at room temperature, 2 to 3 days. Acrylic paints can be used to add color to the design. When completely dry, spray surface with a matte finish to protect and waterproof. When using fresh flower display, place a small plastic container in flower holder to retain water. Dried floral arrangements can be placed directly in flower holder. Place the nail in the sundial hole to cast a time shadow when hung on a sunny wall surface.

Floral Sconce

Fashion a creative floral sconce from the decorative color mesh of your choice. Design a set of 3 and then add a simple, elegant touch to a variety of floral arrangements.

TOOLS & MATERIALS

- Wire cutter
- Silver wire mesh (29 by 8½ inches)
- Old newspaper
- Spray paint
- Decorative trim (9 feet)
- Gauge wire
- Small nails
- Hammer
- Dried flowers, leaves or feathers

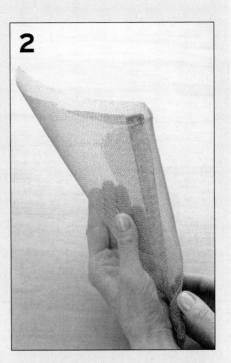

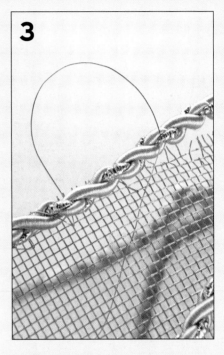

1 Cut 3 pieces from the wire mesh: 11 by 8½ inches, 10 by 7½ inches, and 9 by 6½ inches. Lay these pieces on an old newspaper. Choose a spray paint color to match your room decor. Evenly spray paint one side of the mesh. Allow for drying time, then turn mesh to opposite side and spray color evenly across the mesh.

2 Shape one piece of mesh into a cone shape, tapered at the bottom and fanned out at the top. Turn the seam side to the back, with the tall triangle point in the front. Pinch the bottom of the mesh to keep the cone in place. Take back seam and twist and wrap to hold the shape of the sconce. Repeat this step for the other 2 pieces of wire mesh.

3 Slip one end of decorative trim into the bottom of the sconce, wrapping it in place. Loop the trim around sconce's outer surface drawing up and over front triangle. Use thin gauge wire to secure trim to wire mesh. Weave wire in and out on top of sconce and on several points along the front of sconce, so trim remains secure in place. Repeat this step to finish all 3 sconces. Arrange sconces on a wall and hang by nailing small nails on the back of each sconce, driving nails into the open space of wire mesh into the wall. Make an elegant floral arrangement using dried flowers, leaves or feathers to fill each sconce. Change the arrangement for the seasons or special occasions.

Knitting

An age-old needlecraft, knitting has been enjoying a resurgence in popularity. Today's projects are fast and easy ones that use larger needles, simple patterns and unique specialty yarns. Adding to knitters' choices, many artisans even raise their own animals and spin yarn for themselves or to sell.

Yarns

Yarns are spun from fibers that are either natural (wool, cotton, mohair, angora, linen and silk) or synthetic (acrylic, polyester, rayon and metallic) or a combination of these. In addition, the treatment of the fibers during spinning determines the "look" of the yarn, thus producing specialty yarn variations like Bouclé, Eyelash, Fun Fur or Chenille yarn. Using ribbon for knitting results in a unique look different from yarn.

Knitting patterns list specific types of yarn to use. Each type of yarn has a different thickness or "weight." The five basic types of yarn include baby/fingering (finest), sport weight, worsted weight, chunky and bulky (thickest). Available at craft and discount stores as well as specialty yarn shops, yarn is packaged in balls, skeins (in several variations) or spools (as for ribbon).

The yarn label offers important information including the yarn's fiber content (wool or cotton, for example); the number of ounces/grams or yards in the ball or skein (important if you choose a yarn that's different from the pattern); the yarn's weight type; and the needle size required to achieve a specific gauge (see Gauge on page 137). You may find the term "ply" on labels; this refers to the number of threads that were twisted together to form the yarn strand.

Choose your yarn based on your pattern and the end result you desire.

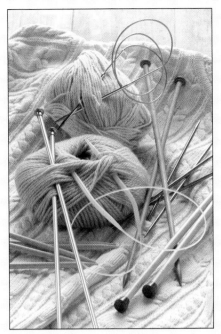

Knitting tools.

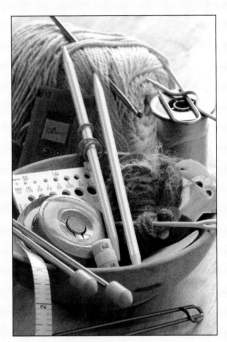

Knitting accessories.

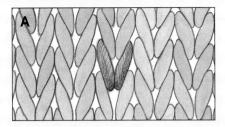

Tools

The most important tools for knitting are the needles, which are either straight or circular. A double-pointed needle is one special type of straight needle used for knitting socks and sometimes mittens. Used for "knitting in the round," circular needles have a needle on each end of a plastic wire. Knitting needles are most commonly made of aluminum, plastic or wood and may be coated with plastic or Teflon. Knitters choose needles by preference based on the way the needles feel during a knitting project. Aluminum needles tend to be "faster" and plastic tends to be quieter. Wood needles work well with natural fibers and are "warm" but work more slowly due to friction.

Most patterns list needle sizes in both American and metric standard. Needle sizes run from very tiny (size 0) to very large (up to size 19 and even larger). Selecting the right size needle will influence your project's outcome. The needle length also varies and is chosen by the width or circumference of the project.

Accessories

Several knitting accessories are either nice to have or necessary for specific patterns. A stitch or needle gauge measures needle size; some include a short ruler to measure the gauge sample. Cable needles are short needles used to hold stitches when you're knitting cables. Stitch markers help keep track of positions where the pattern calls for the stitch to change or to mark the start of a row in circular knitting. Crochet hooks work well for picking up dropped stitches. When you knit with two or more colors, you'll find that yarn bobbins are just the thing to hold each different color yarn. You might also put stitch holders, row counters, point protectors and blunt-tipped yarn needles to good use.

Other accessories you'll need (or want) include a tape measure, straight pins, safety pins, a clipper or small scissors, a bag or basket to hold your project, and a small box or zipper bag to hold small accessories inside your knitting bag.

Knitting Techniques

Two traditional knitting methods are the English method (more descriptively called the "throwing" method) and the continental method (also called the "pick" method). Knitters usually learn one way and stick with it. In both knitting methods, neither hand is dominant. You can knit in either method regardless of whether you're right- or left-handed. Left-handed learners will find it helpful to sit opposite a right-handed teacher and mirror-image the process. If possible, same-handed learners and teachers should sit next to one another.

The basic knitting stitches are the stockinette stitch and the garter stitch. To create the stockinette stitch, knit one row and purl the next. The knit side is smooth (Illus. A) and the purl side is bumpy (Illus. B). For the garter stitch (Illus. C), knit every row; both sides are bumpy.

There are many techniques for achieving these stitches, so if you have learned to knit and this book shows something different, it doesn't mean either way is wrong. Today's beginners will commonly learn throwing. If you are learning to knit, these are probably the most commonly used techniques.

Casting On

The first step in knitting is called casting on. There are a variety of ways to cast on, but these illustrations show the common "long-tail" method. Leave a tail about ½ to 1 inch per stitch to be cast on and make a slip knot on a needle, which you'll hold in your right hand (Illus. D). Hold the yarn with the tail around your left thumb and the working yarn around your left index finger. Palm up, use your other fingers to hold yarn securely in a V (Illus. E). Bring the needle up through the yarn held between your thumb and other fingers (Illus. F), use the needle to grab the front of the strand on your index finger, then go back down through the thumb loop. Drop the loop off of your thumb, returning your thumb to the open V position and tightening the stitch on the needle (Illus. G).

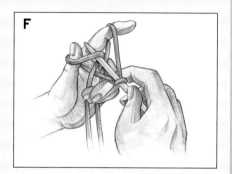

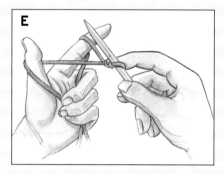

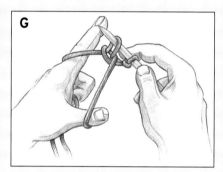

Knitting

To knit using the "throwing" method, cross needles and position yarn behind them. Insert right needle into the first loop on the left needle (right needle is behind left needle). Using your right hand, wrap working yarn behind right point then forward between both points (Illus. H). Grab this strand of yarn by tipping right needle downward; draw the strand down through the loop on the left needle (Illus. I). With the new loop now on the right needle, slide the loop off of the left needle; gently tighten stitch. In patterns, knit is abbreviated K.

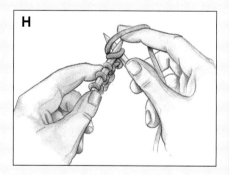

Purling

To purl, cross needles and position yarn in front of them. Insert right needle in front of the first stitch (from right to left) (Illus. J). Using your right hand, wrap working yarn counter-clockwise between needles and around right point (Illus. K). Tipping right needle upward, catch wrapped yarn and draw it through stitch on left needle, creating a loop on right needle and moving right needle behind left (Illus. L). With right needle, slide the loop off of the left needle; gently tighten stitch. In patterns, purl is abbreviated p.

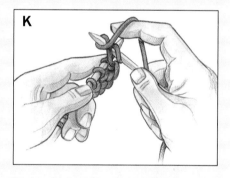

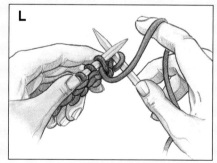

Increasing and Decreasing

Sometimes it is necessary to increase the number of stitches in a row. One way to increase during knitting is to make a knit stitch as usual but do not slip the just-worked stitch off the left needle; work another stitch in that same stitch, inserting the needle into the back of the stitch. Now slip the stitch onto the right needle (Illus. M and N). One way to decrease stitches on your needle is to follow the knit technique, knitting two stitches at once rather than just one (insert right needle into two stitches on left). This technique is abbreviated k2tog (Illus. O and P).

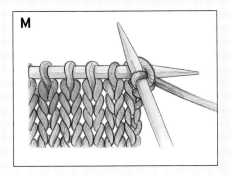

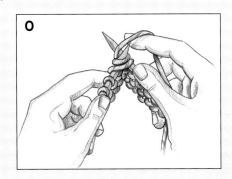

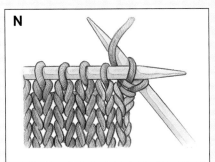

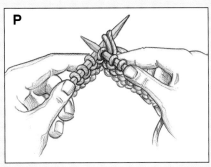

Binding Off

The technique for ending your knitting is called binding off. For a common way to bind off, work the first two stitches of a row to your right needle. Insert left needle into the far right stitch on right needle. Pull this stitch over the stitch closest to the point of the right needle and drop if off the end of the right needle. Knit another stitch from the left needle and repeat the technique until one stitch remains. Remove needle from remaining stitch, snip yarn; then use your fingers to pass the yarn end through the stitch; tug the yarn end to form a knot (Illus. Q, R, S). Using a yarn needle or crochet hook, weave the "tail" of the yarn through the worked stitches.

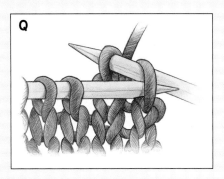

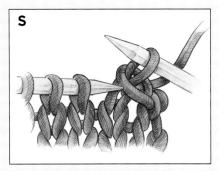

Gauge

In order for your finished project to match the pattern size listed, always calculate your gauge before you start your project. Gauge is the number of rows and stitches you knit per inch. If you knit projects without sizes, such as scarves, you can avoid thinking about the gauge. But once you venture beyond scarves, sooner or later, you will have to check your gauge. To do so, use the pattern's suggested needle size and number of stitches to knit a swatch that is at least 4 inches square. After knitting the swatch, measure 4 inches across it and count the number of stitches. If the recommended number of stitches results in a swatch larger than 4 inches (or if there are fewer stitches than there should be in 4 inches), try again using smaller needle. If the recommended number of stitches results in a swatch smaller than 4 inches (or if there are more stitches than there should be in

4 inches), try again using larger needle. This upfront gauge work may require a swatch or two and may seem tedious, but your end results will be more accurate if you take the time to check your gauge.

Other Considerations

Abbreviations are usually given with every pattern. If you're substituting yarn, ask for help at a yarn shop; changing yarn can affect the gauge.

If you're a beginning knitter, start with an easy pattern and use a plain wool or acrylic yarn. Cotton yarn often splits, and specialty yarns make it difficult to see stitches. Beginning knitters may decide to choose a kit that includes instructions and some basic tools. No matter how a person gets started knitting, many knitters find the activity relaxing and rewarding.

Fancy Scarf

T*his beautiful scarf is worked from length, not width, to give it a new look. The finished size is approximately 50 by 5 inches without the fringe.*

TOOLS & MATERIALS

- Plymouth yarn (Flash, 100% nylon, 50 g (190 yards) per ball, 1 ball lavender (doubled up) No. 96
- Knitting needles (size 15)

- Plymouth yarn (Firenze, 30% wool, 30% acrylic, 40% nylon, 50 g (55 yards) per ball, 1 ball variegated No. 447
- Crochet hook (size G)

1 **For Stitch Gauge:** 8 stitches and 18 rows equals 4 inches garter stitch on size 15 needles.

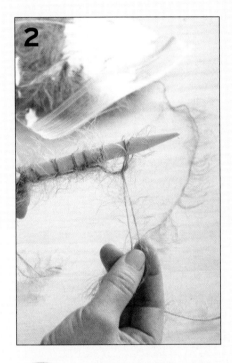

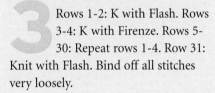

3 Rows 1-2: K with Flash. Rows 3-4: K with Firenze. Rows 5-30: Repeat rows 1-4. Row 31: Knit with Flash. Bind off all stitches very loosely.

2 **For Scarf:** with Flash doubled up, very loosely, cast on 70 stitches. (To cast on loosely: make a slip knot and place it on the needle. Hold the end of the yarn and your needle in your right hand. Wrap the yarn around your left thumb. Insert the needle into the loop. Place the loop on the needle and pull to secure but not too tight.)

4 **To Add Fringe:** cut 16-inch-long pieces of yarn, 2 strands of Flash 1 strand of Firenze; * fold strands in half. Insert crochet hook from back to front into every other stitch and the folded strands (make a loop). Draw end of strands through the loop on the hook; pull slightly to secure. Repeat from *. After fringe on each edge is completed, trim ends evenly.

$

*W*ork these mittens from cuff to fingertip. The only difference between the right and the left mitten is the thumb placement!

TOOLS & MATERIALS

• Bernat Berella "4", worsted weight yarn, 100% acrylic, 3½ oz. per ball, 2 oz. Light Antique Rose No. 08815 (MC = main color), 10 yd. Natural No. 08940

(CC = contrasting color)
• 4 double-pointed knitting needles (size 8)
• Tapestry needle

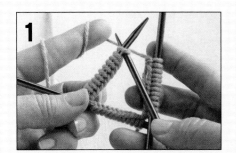

1 **For Stitch Gauge:** 4.5 stitches equals 1-inch stockinette stitch with size 8 needles. **For Right-Hand Cuff:** with MC yarn, cast on 36 stitches on one needle. Divide stitches on 3 needles by moving 12 stitches on each of 2 other double-point needles. Join stitches to make a ring. Avoid twisting stitches. The needle with the beginning tail on the right side is the first needle. **Rounds 1-15:** *K2, p2, repeat from * around. Rounds 16-36: knit around (approximately 3 inches). **For Right-Hand Thumb:** Round 37: K2, with waste yarn knit next 7 stitches. Move all stitches back to left-hand needle and knit them with MC. Knit to end of round. The waste yarn position is where the thumb for mitten will be placed. It will be removed once the main part is finished. For the rest of the hand and fingers: Rounds 38-41: knit around. Rounds 42-43: with CC, knit around. Rounds 44-45: with MC, knit around. Rounds 46-53: repeat rounds 42-45. Rounds 54-61: with MC, knit around (6½ inches from ribbing, or as long as necessary).

2 **To Shape the Top of the Mitten:** Slip 6 stitches from the 2nd needle to the first needle (the needle that starts each round). Slip 3 stitches from the 3rd needle to the

2nd needle. Round 62: (on needle 1): K1, ssk, knit to last 3 stitches, k2tog, k1. On needle 2: K1, ssk, knit to last stitch. On needle 3: Knit to last 3 stitches, k2tog, k1. Round 63: Knit around. Rounds 64-69: Repeat rounds 62-63 (20 stitches remain on all needles). (ssk: Slip first stitch, slip second stitch. Insert left-hand needle into front of both stitches. Knit both stitches together.)

3 **For Top Finishing:** Slip all stitches of needle 3 to needle 2 (10 stitches each on needle 1 and needle 2). Cut yarn about 12 inches long, then thread the tapestry needle. Using tapestry needle graft stitches: With purl sides together, insert tapestry needle into the first stitch on the needle nearest you as if to purl, and leave the stitch on the needle. Pull yarn through. Insert tapestry needle into the first stitch on the far needle as if to knit and leave the stitch on the needle. Pull yarn through. Insert tapestry needle into the first stitch on the near needle as if to knit, slip stitch on to the tapestry needle. Insert into the next stitch on the near needle as if to purl and leave the stitch on the needle. Pull yarn through. Insert tapestry needle into the first stitch on the far needle as if to purl and slip it off the needle onto tapestry needle. Insert tapestry needle

into the next stitch on the far needle as if to knit and leave the needle. Pull yarn through. Repeat steps 3 and 4 until all stitches are off the needle.

4 **For Thumb:** Carefully pull out the waste yarn. You will have raw stitches on both sides. Place these stitches on 2 needles. Needle 1 holds 7 stitches that are closer to the cuff. Needle 2 holds the remaining 6 stitches. On both sides of needle 1, pick up the corner stitch, twist it and place it on needle 2. Move 5 stitches of needle 2 onto needle 3 and 2 stitches of needle 1 to needle 2 so that you now have 5 stitches on each needle. With MC, knit 20 rounds, or as long as necessary. Cut yarn leaving a 6-inch thread. Thread tapestry needle. Pass needle through all stitches and pull tight. Secure the end. Weave in all ends.

5 **For Left-Hand Mitten:** Repeat all instructions for right-hand mitten – just replace the following round for the left-hand thumb position. Round 37: K9, with waste yarn knit next 7 stitches. Move all stitches back to left-hand needle and knit them with MC. Knit to end of round.

Baby Poncho

*T*his adorable little baby poncho is amazingly easy to knit. The little hood keeps little heads warm on chilly days, making this snuggly poncho even more practical.

TOOLS & MATERIALS

- Knitting needles (size 8)
- 2 stitch holders
- Scissors
- Red Heart baby sport pompadour, 100% acrylic sport weight yarn (6 oz. per ball), 7 oz. Gumdrop No. 1928

1 **For Stitch Gauge:** 18 stitches equals 4 inches in garter stitch with size 8 needles.

2 **For Front:** Cast on 62 stitches. Knit in garter stitch for 9 inches, slipping the first stitch of each row as if to purl. This will help you work in the fringe. **For neckline opening:** Knit in garter stitch on 24 stitches. Place the stitches on stitch holder. Bind off 14 stitches for the front neckline. Knit the next 24 stitches.

3 **For Left Side of Neckline:** Knit in garter stitch for 3 inches. Place all stitches on stitch holder. For right side of neckline: Knit in garter stitch for 3 inches.

4 **For Back:** Knit the 24 stitches toward the neckline. Cable cast on 14 stitches (To cable cast on: Step 1. Insert needle in between the next 2 stitches. Step 2: Pull yarn through and place on left needle. Step 3: Repeat steps 1 and 2 until you have the necessary number of stitches.) Knit 24 stitches from the stitch holder. Knit in garter stitch for 12 inches. Bind off all stitches loosely.

5 **For Hood:** Cast on 30 stitches and knit garter stitch for 16 inches. Bind off all stitches loosely. Do not cut yarn. With the right side of the hood facing you, pick up 64 stitches and knit 8 rows of the garter stitch. Bind off all stitches loosely.

6 **For Finishing:** Fold the hood in half and sew the seam. Sew the hood in place at the neck opening.

7 **For Fringe:** * Cut 6-inch-long pieces of yarn (2 strands for each fringe). Fold strands in half. Insert crochet hook from back to front into every other stitch and the folded strands (make a loop). Draw the end of the strands through the loop on the hook. Pull slightly to secure. Repeat from *. Work fringe around the outer edge of the poncho. Trim edges evenly.

Sage Sweatshirt

$ $

*T*urn a basic crewneck sweatshirt into a stylish one-of-a-kind jacket. Really! Combine wonderful textured yarns with your established or newfound knitting skills to create the cozy and decorative accents. Use your favorite yarn and create something special!

TOOLS & MATERIALS

- Sweatshirt
- Iron
- Scissors
- Quilting ruler
- Fabric marker
- ½-inch fusible web tape
- Knitting needles (size 10)
- Yarn: Jewel Box chenille yarn Emerald 0009 and ChaCha curly eyelash Vegas
- Yarn needle
- Straight pins
- Matching thread
- Sewing needle
- Hooks and eyes

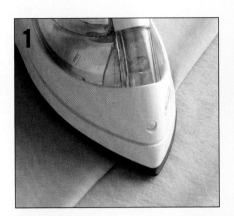

1 Fold the sweatshirt in half lengthwise. Use an iron to press a fold along the center front. Cut along this line. Cut away the ribbing from the bottom of the sweatshirt. Use a ruler to draw a straight line along the bottom edge of the sweatshirt. Cut along this line. Press fusible tape to the inside edges along the front edges and bottom of sweatshirt. Remove backing from fusible web tape and turn over 1 inch to the wrong side along front and bottom; press well. Add additional tape to the ribbing along the neckline.

2 **Collar:** Cast on 70 stitches using both yarns as one. Rows 1 and 2: Knit using both yarns. Row 3: Knit 5 using both yarns, drop eyelash yarn, and continue with chenille only in a P5, K5 pattern until the last 5 stitches. Tie on a 3-foot section of eyelash yarn and purl the last 5 stitches. Continue the next 12 rows in the same pattern adding the eyelash yarn to the first, and last 5 stitches in each row. Cast off using the chenille yarn.

3 **Cuff:** Cast on 32 stitches using both yarns as one. Rows 1 and 2: Knit using both yarns. Rows 3-10: Chenille yarn only, K2, P2, repeat until the end of the row. Cast off. Repeat for second cuff.

4 **Pocket:** Cast on 24 stitches using both yarns as one. Rows 1 and 2: Knit using both yarns. Row 3: Knit 2 using both yarns, drop eyelash yarn and continue with chenille only in a P5, K5 pattern until the last 2 stitches. Tie on a 3-foot section of eyelash yarn and purl the last 2 stitches. Continue the next 20 rows in the same pattern adding the eyelash yarn to the first 2 and last 2 stitches in each row. Knit the final 2 rows using both yarns. Cast off.

5 Tie off any yarn ends and trim. Use the yarn needle to weave yarn ends hiding them among the stitches on the finished collar, cuff and pocket. Pin the knitted collar over the ribbed binding along the sweatshirt neckline. Use matching thread and needle to sew the collar in place. Use a section of yarn and the yarn needle to sew the cuff edges together. Pin knitted cuffs over the ribbed cuffs on the sweatshirt. Use matching thread to sew in place at the top and bottom of cuff edges. Pin the pocket in place on the jacket front. Use matching thread and needle to attach pocket to sweatshirt.

6 **Bobbles:** Cast on 4 stitches using chenille yarn. Rows 2 through 5: K1, P1, K1, P1. Measure approximately 10 inches from knitting needle and cut yarn. Thread yarn needle with yarn. Insert threaded yarn needle back through stitches on the knitting needle, sliding stitches off of the knitting needle and onto the yarn. Weave needle and yarn through the edge of stitches at the side, bottom and up the opposite side of knitted piece. Pull yarn taut, gathering stitches to create a bobble. Finish by tying ends together with an overhand knot. Sew hooks and eyes to the neckline of the sweatshirt as a closure.

Fun "Fur" Hat

Make a simple knit hat with lots of detail and plenty of pizzazz. Knit on circular needles and with two interesting yarns, it is easy to achieve this look. You can make two scarves from skein A and many more projects from skein B. Yarn B is great to use on the edge of almost any project.

TOOLS & MATERIALS

- Size 11 circular knitting needles (29 inches long)
- 1 skein Homespun yarn (yarn A)
- 1 skein Eyelash or Fun Fur yarn (yarn B)
- Stitch marker
- Tape measure or ruler
- Scissors
- Yarn needle

1 Check your gauge: Knit a 5- by 2-inch square with yarn A. Measure 4 inches across knitting and count the number of stitches. The gauge should be 4 inches equal 12 stitches. If it is not, adjust by using larger or smaller needles as needed.

2 Leaving a tail of approximately 4 yards, cast on 72 stitches with yarn A. Make a circle of the needles being careful not to twist the stitches, and put a stitch marker on the right needle. To start knitting, form a knit stitch into the yarn on the left needle. K2, P2, around knitting to marker. Slide marker to other needle and continue in this manner until piece measures 1½ inches. Knit next row.

3 Add yarn B. You will be purling the next rows, so position needles as to purl and place yarn B next to yarn A, leaving a 6-inch tail. Purl each row until the piece measures 1 inch. Drop yarn B, but do not cut. Place yarn B to the inside of circle. Knit next rows for 1½ inches, with yarn A. At the end of every other row bring yarn B around yarn A to catch the yarn. After knitting 1½ inches, add yarn B, as above, and purl each row for 1 inch. Drop yarn B, leave a 6-inch tail, then break the yarn. Knit each row for 1½ inches, with yarn A only.

4 Start the decrease for the crown. Row 1: K6 and K2 together. Row 2: K5 and K2 together. Row 3: K4 and K2 together, repeat until end of row. Row 4: K3 and K2 together, repeat until end of row. Row 5: K2 together, repeat until end of row. This should equal 18 stitches. When you get to rows 4 and 5, pull the flexible part of the needle out between stitches to be able to knit the small circle. This is a bit difficult. Thread tail through a yarn needle and move the stitches, a few at a time, to the yarn needle. When all stitches are on needle, pull stitches tight, closing the hole at the crown. From the inside of the hat, take a few overhand stitches and tie a few knots. Repeat for more strength. Thread extra yarn through a few stitches and cut extra. Do the same with the ends of yarn B.

Evening Bag

This elegant evening bag lets you combine basic knitting skills and decorative design to express your own creative side. This project is so easy you can knit and decorate in the afternoon, then wear it out for a dazzling evening event.

TOOLS & MATERIALS

- Knitting needles (size 10½)
- Chenille yarn (50 yards)
- Ruler
- Scotch tape
- Decorative twine (9 feet)

- Pins
- Thread
- Needle
- Buttons, charms, or beads
- Scissors

1 Using knitting needles, cast on 12 stitches. Knit the first row continuing on into the next row using either a garter stitch or purl stitch. Control the tension of the yarn to keep a tight knit. Knit to a measure of 11 inches in length.

2 Knit the next 12 rows by decreasing a stitch each row. This shapes the top of the bag to fold over. Bind off at the last stitch and knot the end. Leave a 4-inch length of yarn to make a loop for the bag closure. Fold the knit piece into thirds, so that the decreased knit section folds over a doubled knit section.

3 Scotch tape the end of a piece of twine. This will help to guide twine in and out of yarn. Measure one piece of twine to double the length of the side seam of the bag plus 1 inch. Cut and weave in and out of side seam, starting at the top and weaving back down again. Tie a knot of the two ends inside of the bag. Repeat this step to stitch close the second side of the bag. Bow tie a small length of twine to form a closure for the bag. Take extra length of yarn left for loop to wrap around the closure. Tie off and knot. Again Scotch tape one end of the twine. From underside of bag top, loop twine in and out of yarn to creatively design the bag's cover. Use pins to keep design in place. Thread needle and sew small point stitches to keep design in place. Remove pins. Sew additional buttons, charms or beads to complete the bag design. Determine the length of shoulder or hand strap for the bag. Cut this length of twine and tie onto twine stitches on the side of the bag. Connect into top of bag and tie off at opposite side of twine stitch.

*C*reate this elegant yet simple throw pillow. Although the pattern looks complicated, you only work with one color yarn on each row. Reverse the yarn color on the other side for a different look.

TOOLS & MATERIALS

- Knitting needles (size 8)
- Bernat Berella "4," Worsted weight yarn, 100% acrylic, 3½ oz. per ball, 1 ball each Natural No. 08940, Soft Teal No. 1205
- Crochet hook (size G)
- 12-inch pillow form

1 **For Stitch Gauge:** 16 stitches equals 4 inches in stockinette stitch with size 8 needles.

2 **Pattern Instructions:** Multiple of 4 stitches +7. Row 1: with MC (main color), knit through the row. Row 2: Purl through the row. Row 3: with CC (contrasting color), K3, *Sl1 with yarn in back, K3; repeat from *. (Sl1: slip one stitch as if to purl).

3 Row 4: K3, *Sl1 with yarn in front, K3; repeat from *. Rows 5-6: With MC, repeat rows 1-2. Row 7: With CC, K1, *Sl1 with yarn in back, K3; repeat from *. End with K1. Row 8: K1, *Sl1 with yarn in front, K3; repeat from *. End with K1. Repeat rows 1-8 for pattern.

4 **Pillow Instructions:** Cast on 51 stitches. Follow instructions for the front piece until you have 12 inches. Bind off stitches loosely. Knit another piece for the back piece following the same instructions, but reversing the main color and contrasting color.

5 **For Finishing:** With the yarn and crochet hook, work one row of single crochet on three sides of the pillow cover. Insert the pillow shape inside the cover, then join the front and back the same way as the other sides.

Candle and Soap Making

For centuries, people have been making candles and soap by the same basic processes we use now.

Supplies have changed, making processes easier or more convenient and improving options. Today these crafts hold a bit of allure, as candles and soap appeal to our senses and make good gifts. Craft stores usually have a good selection of supplies needed for both crafts.

Candle Making

Limited only by our imaginations, candle making variations are practically endless. Candle styles include rolled candles, dipped candles, molded candles and decorated candles.

Waxes and Candle Molds

Glycerin-based wax is the most popular wax sold in craft stores. Paraffin wax, which is odorless and colorless, comes in pellet or block form. For quick candle making, try candle gel (for creating candles in glass containers) or candle sand, both of which usually come with everything you need to make your own candle.

Beeswax, the oldest type of wax known, has a nice smell and texture and will extend a candle's burning time. The natural color of beeswax varies from light yellow to deep brown. You may also buy beeswax in bleached white. Beeswax sheets roll easily into candles. Beeswax blocks are more difficult to use because beeswax is so sticky. Without a releasing agent, beeswax is difficult to remove from a candle mold. Candle molds can be made of glass, plastic, rubber or metal. If you're using a household item for a mold, pay attention to its top opening. In order

Basic candle making materials and numerous specialty products are available in craft stores.

for the candle to be removed from the mold, the opening must be larger than the rest of the mold. Try using old tins, jam jars, sand pails, cookie cutters or muffin tins. Commercially manufactured rubber molds are available in fun

138

and intricate shapes. The flexible nature of these molds allows candles to be removed without using stearin, which causes wax to shrink. Although they're costly, rubber molds are worthwhile if you want to make a large quantity of candles at once.

Wicks and Other Materials

Wicks, made of flat braided cotton, are usually dipped in a chemical to retard burning. They come in small, medium and large diameter. The size you use will depend on the size of the candle. Wick supports are also used with most candle projects. You'll use a wicking needle—available in 4- to 10-inch lengths—for threading wicks through candles and piercing and threading wicks into molds.

Additional candle making materials include stearin and mold seal. If you work with paraffin wax, you'll use stearin (in white pellet form). In addition to causing shrinkage, it also makes the candle burn longer and the wax more opaque. A mold releasing spray can also be used to make it easier to remove the candle from the mold. Other additives include luster crystals (for sheen) and Snow Way for opaqueness and high luster. Mold seal is a putty used to make candle molds watertight around the hole where the wick goes through the bottom of the mold.

Add color to wax with dye chips, color squares or liquid, specifically for candle making. To make scented candles, add scented oils, scented liquid or scent squares to the wax, or stir in fresh or dried herbs or flowers. Use rubber or glass molds, as scented oils will damage plastic molds. You can purchase a starter kit that includes items needed to make scented candles.

Additional candle making tools.

Options for making decorative candles are endless. Try layering colors, adding corrugated cardboard around the mold or adding ices cubes before pouring the wax. After removing a candle from the mold, you can decorate its surface. Consider adding pebbles, decorative tacks, leaves or beads to a homemade or purchased candle's surface. Or paint, emboss or gild your candle. Use your imagination and get creative!

Candle making tools are worth the investment.

Equipment and Tools

For a heat source, it is safest to use a unit separate from your stove; a hot plate works well. You'll need a double boiler, or you can purchase a specialized melting pot. A metal dipping can is ideal for holding hot wax, especially when you're making dipped candles. A kitchen scale works well to weigh materials to exact measurements as required. A special wax thermometer—covering a range of 100 to 350 degrees F—is recommended.

A few miscellaneous items will be valuable during your process of making candles. Use an old wooden spoon to stir dye into melted wax. You'll want to keep wax paper handy and an old baking sheet, onto which you'll pour surplus wax. Use a small kitchen weight to hold a full mold down in its water bath.

Soap Making

Soap is made three different ways: melt-and-pour, cold-processing (from scratch) and rebatching. Each method involves different levels of technical skill and different ingredients. For all methods, you can experiment with color and fragrance.

Melt-and-Pour

The melt-and-pour method is least technical and allows for more design creativity. This method involves cutting up or grating transparent or opaque glycerin soap and melting it in a double boiler or a microwave. Most craft stores offer a selection of glycerin soap in clear, opaque or with additives like avocado, cucumber or olive oil. You may add fragrance or color or almost any item—coffee beans or a hidden toy, for example—to melt-and-pour soap.

To make melt-and-pour soap, you'll need cooking spray, a disposable chopstick, glycerin melt-and-pour soap base, a heat-resistant glass measuring

Soap making doesn't require specialty tools or materials.

cup, a kitchen knife that's not serrated, a stove or microwave, soap molds and a deep skillet (not shown).

Cold-Process

The traditional way of soap making, cold-processing is the most time consuming and technical method. Cold-processing calls for a combination of fats mixed with a lye solution. You must follow a formula that includes the specific type of fat to use and its ratio to lye. The goat milk shaving soap project uses the cold-processing technique.

Rebatching

Rebatching involves combining freshly grated cold-process soap (purchased or homemade) with liquid, such as water or milk. Rebatching is easier, less messy and less caustic than starting from scratch. Rebatching also offers a way for you to divide a batch of homemade soap into smaller batches that feature various colors, scents or botanicals.

To make rebatched soap, you will need cooking spray, a cooling rack, a crockpot or covered casserole dish, a cutting board, unscented grated soap, a kitchen knife that's not serrated, liquid (water, infused water or milk), soap molds, an oven, a plastic spatula and a wooden spoon.

Containers and Additives

You'll need a container in which to let your soap set. You can use a household container like a loaf pan, polyvinyl chloride (PVC) pipe section or muffin tin. For the cold-process method, a shoebox lined with a plastic garbage bag works well. You can purchase molds specifically for soap or use candle molds, candy molds, plaster molds or metal tart shells. (Most of these work best with the melt-and-pour method.) Wooden soap molds with lids are available, but they are expensive.

In any of the methods, you may use colorant, scents, botanicals and other additives, all of which you can find at your craft store. Always add a colorant before adding scented oil. You can puchase soap colorants or dyes in powder, tablet, grated or liquid forms. (Liquid is easiest to use.) Natural pigments may also be added; take care not to breathe these fine powders. You may add herbs or spices, such as instant coffee or tea, kelp, cocoa or cinnamon. To layer different colors, first spray the soap with rubbing alcohol to make sure the layers bond.

To make scented soap, use essential oils or fragrance oils. To ensure your oils are suitable for cold-process, buy them in the soap making section of craft stores and check labels. Botanicals like rosebuds, lavender, oatmeal, green tea and rosemary are generally added for their beneficial properties or visual appeal rather than for scent. Do not use room scenting oils or potpourri in your soap.

Safety is important both when making candles and making soap because both require a heat source, or lye and working with very hot liquids. Do not leave your work unattended. Keep children and pets away from your work area when using anything hot or caustic. Some soap making uses lye, which is caustic and requires good ventilation. Use of safety glasses and rubber gloves is also necessary when working with lye.

Do not pour unwanted wax or soap down the drain. If wax spills, allow it to solidify and then remove it.

Soap making additives bring aroma, texture and color to your creations.

Goat Milk Shaving Soap

*H*omemade soap is great for shaving and makes a wonderful gift for any man. The natural process of saponification creates glycerin, which makes a very slippery shaving surface and also moisturizes the skin wonderfully.

TOOLS & MATERIALS

- Olive oil (24 oz.)
- Palm oil (12 oz.)
- Coconut oil (12 oz.)
- Plastic mixing bowl with pour spout
- Microwave oven
- Distilled water (18 oz.)
- Glass measuring cup (at least 2-cup size)
- Lewis Red Devil Lye (6.1 oz.)
- Ice bath or sink
- Two kitchen thermometers (must measure down to 100°F)

- Goat milk (4 oz.)
- Plastic spatula
- Electric blender stick
- Plastic measuring containers
- Plastic cups and lids or plastic wrap
- Camping cooler
- Hot water bottles
- Wire rack
- Plastic or wood filler for cup bottom
- Shaving brush and cup

1 Place oils into large plastic mixing bowl. Heat oil just to the melting point, mix, and set aside. Pour distilled water into measuring cup. Place cup in a well-vented area such as under a range hood set at high speed. Slowly pour lye crystals into distilled water until the lye solution is clear.

2 Place lye solution and oil mixture in ice water bath; cool to temperature of 105 degrees F. (Since the lye solution will be hotter, it should go into the cold water bath first.)

Add 4 ounces of goat milk to the oil just after it reaches 105 degrees. Pour lye solution slowly into the oil while mixing with a spatula. When lye solution is completely poured in, switch to the electric blender stick. Check for tracing every few minutes until the soap reaches the trace point. Pour the raw soap into a small plastic cup.

For shaving soap, use a round plastic cup with a smaller radius than the shaving cup you intend to use. Cover the cup tightly with plastic wrap or the cup lid and place it in a warmed camping cooler filled with hot water bottles. Close lid of cooler tightly and leave the soap to process for 24 hours.

3 After soap processes for 24 hours, remove it from the warm cooler and place it in the freezer for two hours or until soap is frozen solid. Remove soap from the freezer and force the soap from the container by flexing the plastic and holding the cup upside down.

Place the soap on a wire rack in a cool dry place to allow drying and hardening. Don't use soap for 2 to 4 weeks to ensure it is completely processed and will stay hard after use. After soap is hard, place small filler in the bottom of a cup and place the soap on top of the filler. The filler keeps the soap out of water added during the brush and lather process. Water can be poured out of the cup allowing the soap to remain dry after each use.

Soap Petals

*D*ip silk or artificial flower petals and leaves in scented clear glycerin soap. Then place them in a bowl or basket for a special touch in the guest bathroom or your own. Each soap petal or leaf can be used once and then discarded. Package in netting or a sheer bag and give as a gift.

TOOLS & MATERIALS

- Scissors
- Artificial flower bush (new or used)
- Bowl
- Clear glycerin soap
- 2 microwaveable bowls
- Microwave
- Soap fragrance
- Toothpicks
- Tweezers
- Wax paper
- Knife
- Netting, tulle or sheer gift bag
- ½-inch-wide ribbon or lace

1

2

3

1 Cut medium-sized petals and leaves from flower bush and place in bowl.

2 Put a small block of glycerin soap in sturdy microwaveable bowl. Melt according to manufacturer's instructions. Add drops of fragrance following manufacturer's directions and stir with a toothpick. Using tweezers, pick up a petal or leaf along the base and edge and dip briefly to cover, into the melted soap. Pull petal or leaf out of soap and let drip briefly.

3 Place petals on wax paper. Let solidify approximately 10 to 15 minutes. Run a knife under petals to easily remove them from the freezer paper. For gifts, wrap soap petals gently in netting and secure with ribbon.

*D*elicate rose blossoms adorn the front of a simple peach candle. Create the illusion of intricately carved petals that will have everyone envious of your new-found skill. These make wonderful and inexpensive table accents.

TOOLS & MATERIALS

- Air dry modeling compound (white)
- Mini leaf clay cutter
- Fresh leaf
- Water-based super glue
- Candles
- Scissors

1 To make the roses and leaves: Pinch ¼-inch ball of modeling compound into a rounded teardrop shape between your thumb and index finger. Take the time to thin the edges. Rosebuds use 2 to 3 petals, roses use 5 to 7.

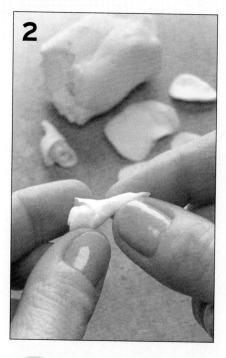

2 Tightly roll a single petal shape for rose center. Add three more petals, slightly overlapping each, working around the center. Flare petal edges outward slightly. As each row of petals is added, move down the rolled center to achieve a more balanced look. Continue adding petals until rose is desired size. Pinch off any excess compound from the bottom. Let air dry.

3 Press a 1-inch ball of compound to ⅛ inch thick. Use the clay cutter to cut out leaves. Press the back of the fresh leaf into the cut-out leaf. Remove leaf and pinch ends to a point. Let air dry.

4 Roll a small amount of modeling compound into a thin rope 1 to 2 inches long. Twist and curl the rope upon itself. Let air dry.

5 Glue completed flowers, leaves and curls to the front of the candle in a pleasing arrangement. Use scissors to trim away excess compound from the back of flowers if necessary.

Candle Dressing

*C*andles become common-
place only if you let
them. They don't have to
be plain! Dress up any candle
with beautiful embellishments for
a pleasing look.

TOOLS & MATERIALS

- Scrapbooking scissors with deckle edge
- Striped scrapbooking paper (12 by 12 inches)
- Large candle
- Tape
- White glue
- 1 yard (2½-inch wired) striped ribbon
- Hot glue gun
- Wire cutters
- 1 silk gerbera daisy
- Artificial grapevine/grapes
- Florist tape
- 6 T-pins
- 6 (8-inch) twigs

1 Using deckle-edge scissors, cut 2 long strips from the scrapbooking paper, approximately 1 inch less than the height of the candle. Tape strips together from underneath, matching their pattern if possible. Glue front flap down. Wrap long paper strip around the middle of the candle, and tape in place.

2 Wrap ribbon around the candle, and cut it with a 1-inch overlap. With a dot of hot glue, hot-glue the ribbon together. Using wire cutter, cut ends of the flower and grapevine stems down to about 2 inches long. Join the flower and the top grapevine stem and wrap approximately 12 inches of florist tape around their stems, pulling the florist tape taut. At the end of the tape, press

it hard into itself and it will hold. Place the bottom grapevine below the flower, and wrap approximately 12 inches of florist tape around their stems, pulling the florist tape taut. At the end of the tape, press it hard into itself and it will hold. Using 2 T-pins, pin this flower/grapevine "corsage" into the side of candle where the ribbon ends meet, making sure to keep the artificial leaves away from the top of the candle.

3 Using florist tape, tape together 2 bundles of twigs, approximately 8 inches long. Using 2 T-pins per bundle, pin them into the side of the candle, underneath the flower and grapevines, one above, and one below, the flower/grapevine.

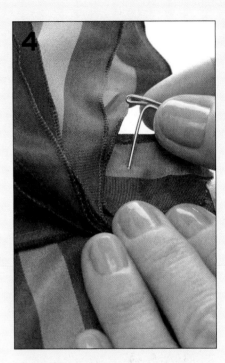

4 With the remaining ribbon, make 3 ribbon loops. With a line of hot glue, glue the ends together, forming a ribbon bundle. With a T-pin, pin the ribbon to the underside of the flower/grapevines. Arrange the ribbon into the desired shape.

149

Candles produce a wonderful mood whenever they are used. So when you travel, take a few along. Palm wax with a crystal finish is created in a handy traveling tin and scented to liven up stuffy rooms. Make travel candles for gifts or for your own personal explorations.

TOOLS & MATERIALS

- 3 tins (2- by 3¼-inch)
- Medium wick, pre-waxed and in wick tab
- Glue dots
- 3 craft sticks with hole drilled in middle
- Crystallizing palm wax – granulated container blend
- Melting pot and saucepan
- Large saucepan
- Water
- Candle-making thermometer
- Concentrated candle dye – blue and green
- 12-inch wooden dowel (stirring stick)
- Candle scents – French, vanilla and lavender
- Wooden skewer
- One sheet each – fabric stickers, in sheet, labels and borders (or other chosen stickers)
- Permanent black pen
- Craft jewelry glue
- 3 silver flower charms
- 3 acrylic 4-mm rhinestones, clear

1 Prepare the tins by adding the wick tab into the center bottom of each tin with a glue dot. Thread the wick through a craft stick and place across the opening making sure the wick is straight and in the center.

2 Place approximately 4 cups wax in the melting pot, then in a large saucepan with water. Insert the candle thermometer and heat wax until melted. Add equal, small shavings of the green and blue coloring to create the soft teal hue. Stir gently until well mixed.

When the temperature is between 160 and 185 degrees F, add approximately one teaspoon each of the lavender and vanilla fragrances. Carefully fill the tins with the molten wax to ½ inch of the top of the mold. Palm wax shrinks very little and as it cools, does not create a depression. Run the skewer along the wick to dispel any trapped bubbles. Let candle wax cool and harden at room temperature. Do not force cool the wax. As the crystallizing wax slowly cools, beautiful crystals will appear on the top.

3 When the candle has completely cooled, add the decorative stickers to the tin to decorate. Make a label by writing the fragrance on a sticker. Top the tin by gluing on the floral charm and rhinestone.

Appendix

DECORATIVE PAINTING
BRUSH CHART

TYPES OF BRUSHES	MEDIUM	USE
Stencil	Misc.	Paper, wood, metal and textile
Round Pointed	Watercolor	Retouching, lettering and wash rendering
Flat	Watercolor	Flat areas and detail
Spotting	Watercolor	Retouching and detail
Bamboo	Watercolor	Ceramic etching, watercolor and fine sketching
Wash	Watercolor	Wash, watercolor, tempera painting and rendering
Soft Hair – Round	Oil	Fine detail in oil, acrylics, ceramics and textiles
Soft Hair – Bright (Short Flat)	Oil	Smooth textural effects
White Bristle – Bright (Short Flat)	Oil	Crisp textured brush effects
White Bristle – Flat (Long Flat)	Oil	Flexible stroke technique
White Bristle – Round	Oil	Sketching, line and detail work
White Bristle – Flibert (Regular)	Oil	Fine and broad strokes
White Bristle – Scenoramic	Oil	Large areas, underpainting and abstract painting
White Bristle Fan	Oil	Delicate or blending effects
Golden Nylon – Flat	Acrylic & Polymer	Acrylic techniques
Golden Nylon – Round	Acrylic & Polymer	For sketching, wash and detail painting
Golden Nylon – Round Pointed	Acrylic & Polymer	Pointed for watercolor and rendering
One Stroke	Tempera	For watercolor, wash, blending, lettering, poster, ceramic glazing, etc.
Liner	Ceramics	Decorative line and accenting in ceramics and oil
Script	Ceramics	Script and brush strokes

SEWING DECOR AND CRAFTS
MACHINE NEEDLE SIZE

SINGER	METRIC
11-14	75-90
14-18	90-100
16-19	100-120
18-21	110-130
19-22	120-140
21-23	130-160

CHOOSE NEEDLE SIZE BY FABRIC WEIGHT

SINGER	METRIC	FABRIC
8	60	Lightweight fabric: challis, chiffon, foulard, dotted Swiss and crinoline
10	80	Medium-weight fabric: jersey, lycra, linen or calf leather
11-14	75-90	
14-18	90-100	Heavy fabrics: vinyl, upholstery or canvas
16-19	100-120	
18-21	110-130	Very heavy fabric

Paper Crafts and Scrapbooking

TYPES OF PAPER

PAPER TYPE	SUGGESTED USE
Canvas	Printer friendly, fast-drying and verstile (easily hand-colored with pencil, markers or chalk)
Metallic	Adds shimmer and shine
Cork and Burlap	Use for adding creative accents (rip the cork and cut and fray the burlap)
Velveteen	Adds richness and elegance. Use for matting photographs
Laser Mulberry	Use for invations or cards
Natural Handmade	Thicker paper embellished with unique elements (leaves, flowers, etc.)
Double-Sided Mulberry Cardstock	Double-sided with complimentary colors
Brocade	Thicker than Mulberry. Unique finishes may contain dried elements

Jewelry and Beading

APPROXIMATE NUMBER OF BEADS PER INCH

BEAD SIZE	BEADS PER INCH	7" STRAND	18" STRAND	24" STRAND
11	19	133	342	456
15	25	175	450	600
Delicas	20	140	360	480
6	10	70	180	240
2mm	13	91	234	312
3mm	8.5	59.5	153	204
4mm	6.5	45.5	117	156
6mm	4	28	72	96
8mm	3	21	54	72
10mm	2.5	17.5	45	60

MEASUREMENTS OF SEED BEADS

SIZE	MILLIMETERS	INCHES
6°	3.7mm	0.145
8°	3.0mm	0.118
11°	2.2mm	0.087
15°	1.5mm	0.059

SUGGESTED ARRANGEMENT FLOWERS

FLOWER TYPE	DESCRIPTION
Bishop's lace (*Ammi majus*)	Think of Queen Anne's Lace, only bigger. Snow-white, 6-inch blossoms on long, graceful stems.
Bachelor's buttons, ragged sailor, or bluet (*Centaurea cyanus*)	Classic heirloom flowers with thistle-shaped blossoms. Try 'Blue Boy', brought to America in the 17th century and cultivated by Thomas Jefferson. This self-seeding annual is 2 to 3 inches tall and extremely easy to grow.
Bells of Ireland (*Molluccella laevis*)	This long-time favorite has been cultivated since 1570. It's very easy to grow; and you can use its flowers fresh or dried About 2 feet tall.
Calendula or pot marigold (*Calendula officinalis*)	All calendulas open with the sun and close as it wanes, a characteristic noted by Shakespeare. Try Pacific Beauty mix (4-inch flowers) or 'Radio', which was introduced in the 1930s and grows 18 to 24 inches tall.
Cleome or spider plant (*Cleome hassleriana*)	Cleome was introduced to England from the West Indies in 1817. This self-seeding annual is 3 to 4 feet tall and comes in white, pink, violet, or rose.
Cockscomb (*Celosia cristata*)	What could be more Victorian than these plush velvet blooms? They were introduced to Europe late in the 16th century, and Thomas Jefferson planted them at his boyhood home. Start indoors in spring. Easy to transplant, they get about 18 inches tall.
Coleus (*Coleus bluemei*)	A stunning foliage plant with colors ranging from red to green to purple. Try the Rainbow mix, which offers a variety of color combinations on large, sturdy plants, about 18 to 20 inches tall.
Cosmos (*Cosmos bipinnatus*)	The Sensation mixture is one of the earliest-blooming cosmos mixtures. These 4- to 5-foot-tall plants are sturdy with ferny foliage. In 1936, this was an All America Selections winner.
Kiss-me-over-the-garden-gate (*Polygonum orientale*)	Also called ladyfingers. This plant came to America in 1737, and its ample self-sowing has ensured its survival ever since. The dangling blooms of deep rose cascade from a 6- to 7-foot-tall plant. Nice as a fresh or dried flower.
Love lies bleeding (*Amaranthus caudatus*)	Long, rope-like, wine-red blooms. Good for fresh or dried bouquets. A self-seeder that grows 3 to 5 feet tall.
Nicotiana, night-scented tobacco, or woodland tobacco (*Nicotiana sylvestris*)	The front-page star of Park Seed's 1904 Floral Guide, this tall plant with fragrant flowers is still a stunning beauty. This self-seeder grows 4 to 5 feet tall.
Snapdragon (*Antirrhinum majus*)	Go for mixtures of tall varieties in a brilliant range of colors—from red to yellow to lavender. These easy-to-grow flowers produce majestic spikes of bloom on thick, sturdy stems.
Stock (*Matthiola longipetala*)	Try 'Starlight Scentsation', an old-fashioned fragrant favorite in a variety of pastel colors. These 18-inch plants look great in containers.
Sunflower (*Helianthus annus*)	There are many great sunflowers available. The flowers of 'Autumn Beauty' range from bright yellow to gold to dark burgundy. It grows 5 to 8 feet tall. 'Evening Sun' has beautiful, large flowers with an extremely dark center. The plants are 6 to 8 feet tall. 'Mexican Sunflower' or 'Torch' (*Tithonia rotundifolia*) has brilliant red-orange 2- to 3-inch blossoms and grows 5 feet tall. The masses of blooms attract butterflies.
Verbena (*Verbena bonariensis*)	Introduced to England from South America in 1726, this 4-foot-tall verbena has clusters of deep lilac flowers in rounded heads. A tender perennial, it is usually grown as an annual. It self-seeds easily.
Zinnia (*Zinnia elegans*)	'Benary's Giant' is a striking, large-flowered strain of zinnia from one of the oldest German seed companies. Blooms are 4 to 5 inches across, come in a wide range of colors, and are fully double. Its extra-long stems make it a great cut flower.

KNITTING

KNITTING NEEDLE CONVERSIONS

US	METRIC
0	2mm
1	2.25mm
2	2.5mm
3	3mm
4	3.5mm
5	3.75mm
6	4mm
7	4.5mm
8	5mm
9	5.5mm
10	6mm
10 1/2	6, 7, 7.5mm
11	8mm
13	9mm
15	10mm
17	12.75mm
19	16mm
35	19mm

YARN SIZES AND SUBSTITUTIONS

YARN TYPE	USUAL GAUGE PER INCH	SUGGESTED NEEDLE SIZE
Ultrafine (Lace or Baby Weight)	8+	00-2 2-3mm
Fine (Fingering Weight)	6-8	2-4 3-3.75mm
Medium (Sport Weight)	5-6	4-6 3.75-4.5mm
Heavy (Worsted Weight)	4-5	7-9 5-6mm
Bulky	3-4	10-10 1/2 6.5-7.5mm
Very Bulky (or Super Bulky)	2-3	13-15 9-10mm

CANDLE AND SOAP MAKING

TYPES OF CANDLES

Molded Candle	Any candle made by pouring motlen wax into a mold and then released
Container Candle	Wax poured into a metal, glass, or pottery container with a wick and is not unmolded
Votive Candle	A small freestanding candle, made with the molded method
Pillar Candle	A larger freestanding candle, can be made with the rolled beeswax or molded methods
Taper Candle	A slender candle used in a holder; can be made with the rolled beeswax, dipped, or molded methods
Tea-Light candle	A small cylindrical candle in aluminum or polycarbonate holder
Hurricane Candle	The outer wax shell of this pillar candle has dried flowers, shells, or other embedded items; designed to burn down the middle, illuminating the outer shell

TYPES OF WAX

Paraffin	Most widely used wax, derived from oil. Economical with superior qualities; can be layered using different colors to create decorative candles. Paraffin wax is available in slab or pellet form, and comes in a wide array of colors.
Beeswax	Most prestigious and expensive wax. Available in blocks or pellets in either white or (natural) amber. Can be mixed with paraffin; can be difficult to remove from mold if made with pure beeswax. Works best with polycarbonate molds and square braided wick.
Natural Wax	Recently popular, takes renewable waxes from a variety of sources, including soy, palm, cottonseed, and other vegetables. There are now numerous blends designed for each method. Many natural waxes do not need any additives and experience minimal shrinkage.

Project Index

General Index